GameMaker Programming Challenges

Programming Challenges to Improve Your GML Knowledge

Ben Tyers

Apress®

GameMaker Programming Challenges: Programming Challenges to Improve Your GML Knowledge

Ben Tyers
Worthing, West Sussex, UK

ISBN-13 (pbk): 979-8-8688-2128-8 ISBN-13 (electronic): 979-8-8688-2129-5
https://doi.org/10.1007/979-8-8688-2129-5

Copyright © 2025 by Ben Tyers

This work is subject to copyright. All rights are reserved by the Publisher, whether the whole or part of the material is concerned, specifically the rights of translation, reprinting, reuse of illustrations, recitation, broadcasting, reproduction on microfilms or in any other physical way, and transmission or information storage and retrieval, electronic adaptation, computer software, or by similar or dissimilar methodology now known or hereafter developed.

Trademarked names, logos, and images may appear in this book. Rather than use a trademark symbol with every occurrence of a trademarked name, logo, or image we use the names, logos, and images only in an editorial fashion and to the benefit of the trademark owner, with no intention of infringement of the trademark.

The use in this publication of trade names, trademarks, service marks, and similar terms, even if they are not identified as such, is not to be taken as an expression of opinion as to whether or not they are subject to proprietary rights.

While the advice and information in this book are believed to be true and accurate at the date of publication, neither the authors nor the editors nor the publisher can accept any legal responsibility for any errors or omissions that may be made. The publisher makes no warranty, express or implied, with respect to the material contained herein.

    Managing Director, Apress Media LLC: Welmoed Spahr
    Acquisitions Editor: Spandana Chatterjee
    Editorial Assistant: Gryffin Winkler

Cover designed by eStudioCalamar

Cover image designed by Freepik (www.freepik.com)

Distributed to the book trade worldwide by Springer Science+Business Media New York, 1 New York Plaza, New York, NY 10004. Phone 1-800-SPRINGER, fax (201) 348-4505, e-mail orders-ny@springer-sbm.com, or visit www.springeronline.com. Apress Media, LLC is a Delaware LLC and the sole member (owner) is Springer Science + Business Media Finance Inc (SSBM Finance Inc). SSBM Finance Inc is a **Delaware** corporation.

For information on translations, please e-mail booktranslations@springernature.com; for reprint, paperback, or audio rights, please e-mail bookpermissions@springernature.com.

Apress titles may be purchased in bulk for academic, corporate, or promotional use. eBook versions and licenses are also available for most titles. For more information, reference our Print and eBook Bulk Sales web page at http://www.apress.com/bulk-sales.

Any source code or other supplementary material referenced by the author in this book is available to readers on GitHub. For more detailed information, please visit https://www.apress.com/gp/services/source-code.

If disposing of this product, please recycle the paper

To Dad,

Thanks for buying my first PC – it set me on an interesting path.

Table of Contents

About the Author xxiii

About the Technical Reviewer xxv

Acknowledgments xxvii

Introduction xxix

GameMaker Programming Challenges 1

    1. Keep Instance In Room 2

    2. Line Of Sight.. 3

    3. Simple Level Complete Save System... 4

    4. Seeking Missile 5

    5. Draw Player Health As A Series Of Bars.. 6

    6. Ellipse Movement.. 7

    7. Draw Contents Of 2D Array 8

    8. Adaptable Engine Noise 9

    9. Draggable Objects 10

    10. Mini Map 11

    11. Trail Effect 12

    12. Change Image On Interaction... 13

    13. Mouse Pointer Point Direction.. 14

    14. Power Up... 15

    15. Pushable Block 16

    16. Radar... 17

    17. Random Word From A Text File 18

    18. Real Time Clock Example 19

    19. Score With Leading Zeros 20

TABLE OF CONTENTS

20. Fading Moving Text 21
21. Cool Down System 22
22. Sliding Bar 23
23. Variable Movement Speed 24
24. Rising Smoke Effect 25
25. Typewriter Text Effect 26
26. Level Unlock System 27
27. Weapon Management 28
28. Top Down Character Control 29
29. Blood Effect Using Particles 30
30. Draw Text Info With Background 31
31. Speed Boost 32
32. Projectile Curved Path 33
33. Draw Power Bar With Background 34
34. Create Muzzle Flash 35
35. Cloud Effect Using Effects 36
36. Missile Smoke Trail 37
37. Selectable Stats 38
38. Add Playing Cards & Shuffle 39
39. Enemy Track Player's Movement 40
40. Tool Tip Pop Up 41
41. Pop-Up Wobbly Text 42
42. Grow and Shrink Sprite Control 43
43. Smoothly Move To Mouse Position 44
44. Bounce Off Room Border 45
45. Pause Music When Sound Effect Plays 46
46. Glitch Effect Text 47
47. Wobbly Text 48
48. Choose A Random Instance 49
49. Draw Mini Healthbar 50

TABLE OF CONTENTS

50. Fade In And Out 51
51. Rotating Text 52
52. Flashing Text 53
53. Play Sound At Selected Volume 54
54. Spawn Power-Ups System 55
55. Move Crosshair To Mouse Position 56
56. Checkpoint System 57
57. Check If Instance Is In View 58
58. Jump Through Platforms 59
59. Random Level Music 60
60. Exploding Effect 61
61. Draw Text With Border 62
62. Move Coin To Score Text 63
63. Tire Track Effects 64
64. Fireworks Display 65
65. Spawn Bullets From Double Weapon 66
66. Sprite Drop Shadow 67
67. Simple Top Down Collision 68
68. Spawn Instance With Random Subimage 69
69. Sine Wave Based Movement 70
70. Draw Player's Speed On Dial 71
71. Spawn Trees Border 72
72. One Button Controlled Movement 73
73. Plane Movement 74
74. Player Power Up Creator 75
75. Coin Drop Bonus Effect 76
76. Endless Levels 77
77. Mini Healthbar With Segments 78
78. Outline Shader 79
79. Move Crosshair To Target 80

TABLE OF CONTENTS

80. Spawn Items With Gap 81

81. Add Scores To A List 82

82. Cloud Effect 83

83. Ball Bouncing Off Instances 84

84. Keeping A Value In A Range 85

85. Film Style Scrolling Credits 86

86. Rotate Room View 87

87. Toggle Full Screen 88

88. Progress Bar 89

89. Flash Player To Show Damage 90

90. Fade Between Two Images 91

91. Draw A Path As Circles 92

92. Simple Top Down Control 93

93. Laser To Target 94

94. Bubble Explosion Effect 95

95. Grid Movement Control 96

96. Image Scale, Fade and Rotate Effect 97

97. Player Streak 98

98. Numbers As Text 99

99. Draw Lives As Images 100

100. Coin Explosion Effect 101

101. Follow Object 102

102. Orbit Object 103

103. Random Name Generator 104

104. Top Down Movement 105

105. Screen Shake 106

106. Bomb Destruction Zone 107

107. Circular Healthbar 108

108. Volume Based On Distance 109

109. Snow Weather Effect 110

TABLE OF CONTENTS

110. Password Easter Egg 111
111. Average Position Between 2 Instances 112
112. Random Dice Rolls 113
113. On Screen Keyboard 114
114. Ds List Sort 115
115. Colour Picker 116
116. Numbers To Speech 117
117. Teleport 118
118. Queued Messages 119
119. Shop System 120
120. Parallax Background 121
121. Eight Directional Movement A 122
122. Room Transition Fade In & Out 123
123. Nine Slice Example 124
124. Hit Box A 125
125. Snap To Grid 126
126. Hide & Seek 127
127. Save Highscore 128
128. Sprite Animation Control 129
129. Jet Pack & Gravity 130
130. Enemy Movement On Platform 131
131. Tweening 132
132. Door & Key 133
133. Wrap Instance Around Room 134
134. Change Transparency On Collision 135
135. Weapon Upgrade System 136
136. Knockback 137
137. Road Builder 138
138. Select Multiple Troops 139
139. Road Connections 140

ix

TABLE OF CONTENTS

140. Lightning Effect 141
141. Gravity Movement 142
142. Blood Damage Effect 143
143. Tap Instance To Change Image 144
144. Bullet Holes 145
145. Rope Between Objects 146
146. English to Morse Code 147
147. Loop Through Instances 148
148. Slowly Rotate To Angle 149
149. Draw Clock 150
150. Randomly Place Objects In Room 151
151. Get Text From Keyboard 152
152. Shoot Projectile With Gravity 153
153. Fade On Player Collision 154
154. Jump On Enemy To Kill 155
155. Calculate Size Of Area 156
156. Draw Lines To Mouse Position 157
157. Random Building Generator 158
158. Queue & Play Audio 159
159. Boss Style Movement 160
160. Split Screen 161
161. Check Spelling Of Word 162
162. Player Character Selection A 163
163. Weapon Control & Ammo Packs 164
164. Follow Player At Distance 165
165. Resize Based On Position 166
166. Using Mouse Wheel To Select Weapon 167
167. Font Drawing From Images 168
168. Allow Player To Load Sprite 169
169. Enemy Shoots If Can See Player 170

TABLE OF CONTENTS

170. Randomly Place Instances 171

171. Split Sentence 172

172. Simple Menu System 173

173. Moving Spikes & Damage System 174

174. Projectile Spread System 175

175. Ball Bounce & Squash 176

176. Status Effect 177

177. Footstep Sounds With Animation 178

178. Game Fog 179

179. Destruction With Multiple Subimages 180

180. Enemy Hide 181

181. HUD Drawing On GUI Layer 182

182. Scroll Block Of Text Up and Down 183

183. Blood Spray Effect 184

184. Voice On Level Up 185

185. Wind Blown Effect 186

186. Double Jump 187

187. Meteor Shower Effect 188

188. Footstep Dust Effect 189

189. Float & Die Effect 190

190. Fly Level Effect 191

191. Dash Movement 192

192. Sliding On Ice 193

193. Underwater Effect 194

194. Hint Arrow To Direction Of Powerup 195

195. Button To Open Website 196

196. Health Pack Slowly Increase Health 197

197. Change Enemy Colour When Targeted 198

198. Limit Weapon Shooting Timer 199

199. Clock Stopwatch 200

xi

TABLE OF CONTENTS

200. Weapon Power & Direction System 201
201. Moving A Platform Left and Right 202
202. Spin Around Other Instance 203
203. Vehicle With Smooth Turning 204
204. Tank and Turret Movement 205
205. Bbox Collision 206
206. NPC That Performs Tasks 207
207. Wall Jumping 208
208. Weapon Upgrade System 209
209. Player Shield System 210
210. Sprite Stacking Fake 3D 211
211. Water Reflection Using Effect Layers 212
212. Magnet System 213
213. Health Heart Part System 214
214. Tap To Move System 215
215. Resize Sprite 216
216. Moving Platform Up and Down 217
217. Rotating Wheel 218
218. Fake 3D 219
219. Flame Effect Using Particles 220
220. Rotating Spaceship With Inertia 221
221. Weapon and Manually Select Target 222
222. Destructible Terrain 223
223. Horizontal Scrolling Menu 224
224. Vertical Scrolling Menu 225
225. Ladder Climbing 226
226. Attack Left and Right 227
227. Moving Grass Side View 228
228. Target Enemy With Highest HP 229
229. Rotating Mini Map 230

TABLE OF CONTENTS

230. Screen Flash Damage Indicator 231
231. Board Game Move Pieces A 232
232. Board Game Move Pieces B 233
233. Predict Path Of Projectile 234
234. Animated Mouth When Talking 235
235. Move All Instances By Given Amount 236
236. Split Rocks and Rotate 237
237. Multiple Missiles – Only Target If Not 238
238. Find a Path Through A Maze 239
239. Flying Instance With Shadow 240
240. Cover Whole Room With Instances 241
241. Keyboard Controlled Player With Mouse Controlled Gun 242
242. Spaceship Control 243
243. Slide In Buttons 244
244. Draw Crosshair In Middle Of View 245
245. Draw Rectangle With Dashed Border 246
246. Top Down 360 Degree Movement 247
247. Attacking Sprite Control System 248
248. Enemy Patrol System 249
249. Change Cursor To Selected Item 250
250. Fade Between Text Messages 251
251. Enemy Jumping 252
252. Pick Up and Place Items 253
253. 360 Degree Laser 254
254. Laser Through Multiple Instances 255
255. Draw Sprite On Sprite Layer 256
256. Detect Single Or Double Mouse Button Click 257
257. Leave Path To Attack Then Return To Path 258
258. Choose Random Word 259
259. Change Sprite When Jumping 260

TABLE OF CONTENTS

260. Play Random Sound 261

261. Move Multiple Instances Through A Small Gap 262

262. Draw Text With Formatting 263

263. Moving Grass Top Down 264

264. Turn Before Moving 265

265. Alert Player To Low Health 266

266. Avatar Creator A 267

267. Ship Shooting Cannon Balls 268

268. Simple Glow Effect With Circles 269

269. Simple Glow Effect With Sprite A 270

270. Simple Glow Effect With Sprite B 271

271. Move To Target Then Stop 272

272. Level Based On Score 273

273. Player Control Information 274

274. Selectable Backgrounds 275

275. Draw Buttons With Chosen Language 276

276. Lottery Numbers Selector 277

277. Draw View Border On Draw Event 278

278. Card Flipping Animation 279

279. Day Night Cycle 280

280. Draw Rotating Shapes 281

281. Positional Audio 282

282. Imploding Text Effect 283

283. Laser Collision Effect 284

284. Pop Up Message 285

285. Skill Points 286

286. Depth Based Movement 287

287. Party Mechanics 288

288. Card Battle 289

289. Text Explode 290

TABLE OF CONTENTS

290. Branching Dialogue 291

291. Marquee Text 292

292. Avatar Creator B 293

293. Create Level From Text File 294

294. Enemy Shooting System 295

295. Dropping Effects 296

296. Player Path 297

297. Enemy Movement 298

298. Compass Points 299

299. Drone Weapon 300

300. Old Film Effect 301

301. Weapon Recoil 302

302. Change Cursor 303

303. Swap Music Tracks 304

304. Rotate Sprite With Off Center Origin 305

305. Unlockable Buttons 306

306. Follow Object With Avoidance 307

307. Circular Rotating Text A 308

308. Place Instances Without Blocking Path 309

309. Shooting AI Helper 310

310. Do Something After Given Time 311

311. Extending Frog Tongue Without Sprite 312

312. Extending Frog Tongue With Sprite 313

313. Sprite With Two Attack Modes 314

314. Rotating Tower With Subimages 315

315. Rotate View and Instances 316

316. Reverse Sentence Order 317

317. Generate Random Sentence 318

318. Plane Height and Shadow 319

319. Moon Lander AI 320

xv

TABLE OF CONTENTS

320. Player Character Selection B 321
321. Slowly Reduce Health 322
322. Level Progress - 2 Players 323
323. Find Random Position Outside View 324
324. Recolour Sprite With Blendmode 325
325. Draw Text With Flashing Border 326
326. Count Down Text 327
327. Showing Damage To Spaceship 328
328. Change Volume Of Music 329
329. Slide In Out Stats 330
330. Expanding Rotating Fire Effect 331
331. Move To Position On Sine Wave 332
332. Recoil When Shooting 333
333. Hold Button To Jump Higher 334
334. Choose Random Number 335
335. Iris Effect Room Transition 336
336. Only Show Visible Walls 337
337. Four Directional Dash 338
338. Rectangle Room Transition Effect 339
339. Eight Directional Movement B 340
340. Segmented Neck 341
341. Hold To Change Sprite 342
342. Piece Movement 343
343. Enemy With Trailing Instances 344
344. Reverse Controls 345
345. Four Direction Enemy 346
346. Four Direction Move To Mouse 347
347. Draw Sprite Border 348
348. Keep Crosshair In View 349
349. Safe Password Code 350

350. Morph Between Images 351

351. Rotate Sprite Randomly 352

352. Rotating Stars Effect 353

353. Fade In Out Messages 354

354. Pick Up and Carry 355

355. Bouncing Text Effect 356

356. Motion Blur With Movement 357

357. Draw Sprite To Wall Edge 358

358. Create and Detonate Bomb With Same Button 359

359. Rotatable 3D Car 360

360. Rotatable Ship With Multiple Weapons 361

361. Draw Text With Shadow 362

362. Attacking With Custom Hit Box 363

363. Draw Healthbar From Two Sprites 364

364. Save Players Stats 365

365. Circular Rotating Text B 366

366. Spiralling Weapon 367

367. Selectable Characters 368

368. Proximity Helper 369

369. Temporary Invincibility 370

370. Falling Crates 371

371. Countdown Clock 372

372. Rings Fly Through 373

373. Text Based Menu 374

374. Charge Jump 375

375. Proximity Cone Of Vision 376

376. Instance Selector 377

377. Instance Placer 378

378. Loot Dropper 379

379. Draw Decimal Fraction 380

xvii

TABLE OF CONTENTS

- 380. Stats With Buttons 381
- 381. Show Parts Of A Sentence 382
- 382. Weapon Reload System 383
- 383. Moving Eyes 384
- 384. Audio Control 385
- 385. Prevent Mouse Cursor Moving Over Instance 386
- 386. Directional Shadow 387
- 387. Scale Image 388
- 388. Draw Bounding Box 389
- 389. Poker Hand 390
- 390. Choose and Name Random Playing Card 391
- 391. Fade Sprite In and Out 392
- 392. Circular Healthbar That Adjusts 393
- 393. Dropping Block 394
- 394. Slider 395
- 395. Move To An Instance's Position 396
- 396. Parachute Falling With Wobble 397
- 397. Increasing Difficulty 398
- 398. Incoming Enemy 399
- 399. Warp Portal 400
- 400. Programable Characters 401
- 401. Drawing Sprite Fonts In Different Colours 402
- 402. Stealth Zones 403
- 403. Dynamic Shadows 404
- 404. Proximity Mines 405
- 405. Sticky Projectiles 406
- 406. Reflecting Projectiles 407
- 407. Conveyor Belts 408
- 408. Spreading Fire 409
- 409. Boomerang Mechanic 410

410. Burnable Objects	411
411. Echo Location	412
412. Smooth Dash Movement	413
413. Shock Wave	414
414. Hover Mechanic	415
415. Jumping Pad	416
416. Momentum Jumps	417
417. Gravity Flips	418
418. Explosive Bombs	419
419. Explosive Barrels Chain	420
420. End-of-Level Gate	421
421. Coin Collection	422
422. One Way Blocks	423
423. Wind	424
424. Nuke	425
425. Timed Collectibles	426
426. Retractable Bridge	427
427. Tethering Mechanic	428
428. Squish Image	429
429. Adaptable Button	430
430. Star Effect	431
431. Cracked Walls	432
432. Pressure Plates	433
433. Multiple Weapons	434
434. Camera Pan	435
435. Time-Locked Doors	436
436. Momentum-Based Movement	437
437. Laser Destruction Beam	438
438. Zoom Control	439
439. Teleport Pads	440

TABLE OF CONTENTS

440. Customizable Turrets 441
441. Direction Shield 442
442. Enemy That Circles Player 443
443. Target Enemy With Highest HP 444
444. Cloaking Device 445
445. Enemy Drops 446
446. Rotating Obstacles 447
447. Enemy Patrol Patterns 448
448. Sinking Sands 449
449. Decoy Tools 450
450. Colourful Explosions 451
451. Fighting Game Knockback 452
452. Enemy Mirrors Player 453
453. Random Direction Movement 454
454. Enemy Swoop Attack 455
455. Cluster Bombs 456
456. Synchronized Movement 457
457. Spring-Loaded Enemies 458
458. Gap Crossers 459
459. Slime Trails 460
460. Change Path Direction 461
461. Spiral Dive 462
462. Ambush Hunters 463
463. Healers 464
464. Charging Enemies 465
465. Dodging Enemies 466
466. Orbital Shields 467
467. Swing Enemies 468

468. Hiding Enemies 469

469. Directional Blockers 470

470. Sky Divers 471

471. Split Creatures 472

472. Barrel Rolls 473

473. Dogfight Lock-On 474

474. Cloud Cover Stealth 475

475. Plane Switching 476

476. Colour Matching 477

477. Mine Weapon 478

478. Mini Helper 479

479. Teleporting Enemies 480

480. Patrolling Guards 481

481. Area Explosion 482

482. Mirror Shields 483

483. Harassers 484

484. Spinning Dashers 485

485. Laser Sweepers 486

486. Ground Pounders 487

487. Mini Map Level Selection 488

488. Replenish Stats 489

489. Player Decoy 490

490. Variable Damage 491

491. Solar Flares 492

492. Zombie Enemy 493

493. Surround Player 494

494. Enemy Hint 495

495. Power Upgrade 496

xxi

TABLE OF CONTENTS

496. Electricity Towers **497**

497. Freeze Bullets **498**

498. Money Based Upgrades **499**

499. Random Paths **500**

500. Reinforcement Callers **501**

About the Author

Ben Tyers is an expert GameMaker user, developer, coder, and trainer. He has authored a number of books on GameMaker for game application developers. He has been using GameMaker for over 20 years, enjoying the changes that has happened during this period. Over this time, he has made over 200 mini game projects covering a range of genres, including remakes of retro games he played as child in the 1980s. He loves finding simple solutions to challenging coding concepts. He is an active member of GameMaker's community, helping new coders with programming issues. Outside of programming, Ben enjoys vintage horror and science fiction films.

About the Technical Reviewer

Mark Alexander is a Technical Writer for a AAA gaming company, but in his spare time he makes quirky and fun indie games using the powerful GameMaker engine. Apart from that, he occasionally collaborates with friends on various blogs, administrates the helpful and friendly GameMaker Community support forums, has acted as technical editor on various books for GameMaker, and occasionally indulges in creative photography and writing.

Acknowledgments

Thanks to Mark Overmars for creating the first GameMaker way back in the early 2000s. Also thanks to the opengameart.org community, where I sourced most of the art for the project files that accompany this book.

Introduction

This book contains 500 GameMaker projects to test and increase your GML and game design skills.

Each challenge contains a title, brief explanation, a project outline, useful functions and variables, and a hint on tackling the challenge.

Each challenge also shows a difficulty guide from 1 (easy) to 5 (most challenging). There is also a checkbox you can use to mark if you have completed the challenge.

Difficulty Guides:

- 1 - Only requires a few functions, using examples from the GameMaker Manual should be enough.
- 2 - A little more involved, requires using multiple functions.
- 3 - Challenging concepts that are more involved.
- 4 - Complex functions that require more logic and understanding.
- 5 - Advanced use, provided really as an example of how it can be done.

I have not included a break-down of what the functions and built-in variables do and how they work, you can check-out **GameMaker's Manual** for a description, break-down, and in most cases an example usage:
`https://manual.gamemaker.io/`

GameMaker Programming Challenges

1. Keep Instance In Room

Difficulty 1/5

Project Outline:

To keep x and y values within a certain range to prevent an instance leaving the room borders.

Useful Functions and Built-in Variables:

clamp
keyboard_check

Hints on Tackling This Assignment:

Using clamp you can keep a value within the range of two other given values. Allow keyboard input to change the x and y positions of an instance, using clamp to keep it in the room.

GAMEMAKER PROGRAMMING CHALLENGES

Difficulty
1/5

2. Line Of Sight

Project Outline:

Find a way to detect if there is / is not a crate between the player and an enemy. Draw a line between them if they can see each other.

Useful Functions and Built-in Variables:

collision_line
draw_line
mouse_x
mouse_y

Hints on Tackling This Assignment:

Using collision_line you can set a variable to true or false depending on the collisons status. Set to true when enemy has a direct line of site to a player instance, and draw a line between them. Move the player with the mouse.

3. Simple Level Complete Save System

Difficulty
2/5

Project Outline:

Create a system that save when a level is completed. Use keys 1 to 8 to save.

Useful Functions and Built-in Variables:

ini_open
ini_close
ini_read_real
clamp
ini_write_real
draw_text

Hints on Tackling This Assignment:

Allow some basic input to change a level variable between true and false. Save and load this variable to an ini file. Draw level status using draw_text.

GAMEMAKER PROGRAMMING CHALLENGES

Difficulty
4/5

4. Seeking Missile

Project Outline:

Allow user to click to spawn a missile that flies towards to the position of the nearest enemy, by gradually changing it's flight angle. Destroy enemy and missile upon a successful collision.

Useful Functions and Built-in Variables:

instance_nearest
instance_exists
angle_difference
instance_destroy
instance_create_layer
image_angle

Hints on Tackling This Assignment:

Create a missile upon a mouse click, and change direction gradually to face and target an enemy.

5. Draw Player Health As A Series Of Bars

Difficulty
2/5

Project Outline:

To display visually the players current health as a series of separate bars.

Useful Functions and Built-in Variables:

```
for
draw_rectangle
draw_set_color
health
```

Hints on Tackling This Assignment:

Use the players health and draw rectangles based upon this value. Use a for loop to aid calculating the positions required.

GAMEMAKER PROGRAMMING CHALLENGES

Difficulty
4/5

6. Ellipse Movement

Project Outline:

Use some basic maths to make an instance move around on an elliptical path.

Useful Functions and Built-in Variables:

sin
cos
pi
if
else

Hints on Tackling This Assignment:

Look up some basic trigonometry using the math functions.

7. Draw Contents Of 2D Array

Difficulty 2/5

Project Outline:

To draw a grid containing the data taken from a 2 dimensional array. Populate this array with the 2 times table.

Useful Functions and Built-in Variables:

draw_text
for
draw_rectangle
draw_set_colour

Hints on Tackling This Assignment:

Loop through two for loops by creating a nested loop. Use these values to both access data in the array and to draw it.

GAMEMAKER PROGRAMMING CHALLENGES

Difficulty
2/5

8. Adaptable Engine Noise

Project Outline:

Change the pitch of a playing sound, based on the speed of the player

Useful Functions and Built-in Variables:

clamp
audio_play_sound
audio_sound_pitch
mouse_check_button

Hints on Tackling This Assignment:

Allow user to change a speed value, then set the pitch of the playing sound based on this value.

9. Draggable Objects

Difficulty
2/5

Project Outline:

Allow user to press and hold left mouse button, allowing dragging around the room. If there are 2 or more instances at any position, only allow movement of one of them.

Useful Functions and Built-in Variables:

position_meeting
global
mouse_check_button_*
id

Hints on Tackling This Assignment:

Get an id of a single instance and only allow moving of just that instance. So if two instances are in the same place, only one of them moves.

GAMEMAKER PROGRAMMING CHALLENGES

Difficulty
3/5

10. Mini Map

Project Outline:

Draw a mini map to give player visual info on nearby instances.

Useful Functions and Built-in Variables:

with
if
draw_sprite
draw_rectangle
point_distance
lengthdir_*

Hints on Tackling This Assignment:

Get the distance and direction of instances relative to the player. Use this to draw map sprites using direction and distance (scaled down).

11. Trail Effect

Difficulty
2/5

Project Outline:

Create a trail that remembers (n) previous positions and draws a sprite at those positions with a reduced alpha value based on distance from source.

Useful Functions and Built-in Variables:

array_create
array_delete
array_push
array_length
draw_sprite_ext
mouse_x
mouse_y
for

Hints on Tackling This Assignment:

You can create an array and push in positions of the player. You can also test the length of an array and delete values if above a certain length. Use a for loop to draw a sprite at pevious positions of the player.

12. Change Image On Interaction

Difficulty
1/5

Project Outline:

Change the sub-image of a button based on mouse over, button pressed, or no interaction.

Useful Functions and Built-in Variables:

instance_position
mouse_check_button
image_index

Hints on Tackling This Assignment:

Change the image index of a sprite based on whether mouse is over or not, and if mouse is over and button held down.

13. Mouse Pointer Point Direction

Difficulty 1/5

Project Outline:

Draw a sprite as a pointer that slowly moves to the mouse's position, pointing in the direction of the target position. Hide the default mouse cursor.

Useful Functions and Built-in Variables:

```
move_towards_point
point_direction
window_set_cursor
mouse_x
mouse_y
draw_sprite_ext
```

Hints on Tackling This Assignment:

Get the direction from current position to mouse's position using point_direction Slowly move to the mouse's position.

Difficulty
2/5

14. Power Up

Project Outline:

Change a variable when a key is pressed. Reset the variable after a given amount of time.

Useful Functions and Built-in Variables:

keyboard_check_pressed
alarm
game_get_speed
draw_text

Hints on Tackling This Assignment:

Check for keypress and value, set Alarm and flag accordingly, initially setting powerup to true. When alarm triggers, turn off powerup by setting back to false. Draw state of power up using draw_text.

15. Pushable Block

Difficulty 3/5

Project Outline:

Allow player to push a block when moving.

Useful Functions and Built-in Variables:

place_meeting
mouse_check_button

Hints on Tackling This Assignment:

Move the player with mouse buttons. Move crate if colliding with the player, by checking if player is next to the crate with place_meeting.

GAMEMAKER PROGRAMMING CHALLENGES

Difficulty
3/5

16. Radar

Project Outline:

To create a radar screen and blips of instances near the player.

Useful Functions and Built-in Variables:

with
draw_sprite
draw_rectangle
point_distance
lengthdir_*

Hints on Tackling This Assignment:

Get the distance and direction of instances relative to the player. Draw mini sprites at a fraction of the distance. Draw shapes for the screen.

17. Random Word From A Text File

Difficulty 4/5

Project Outline:

To open and read all words from a text file, and choose one word at random.

Useful Functions and Built-in Variables:

file_text_open_read
file_text_read_string
file_text_readln
file_text_close
file_text_eof

Hints on Tackling This Assignment:

Read words from a text file and store in an array. Read using file_text_read_string and move to next line with file_text_readln. Then choose one entry at random.

GAMEMAKER PROGRAMMING CHALLENGES

Difficulty
2/5

18. Real Time Clock Example

Project Outline:

Grab the players system time and draw as text.

Useful Functions and Built-in Variables:

current_hour
current_minute
current_second
string_repeat
string_length
draw_text

Hints on Tackling This Assignment:

Get current system time, format it with leading 0's as required, and draw on screen Do this by setting variable for hour, minute, and second. Format and draw with draw_text.

Difficulty
1/5

19. Score With Leading Zeros

Project Outline:

To format a score with a given number of leading 0's for example 000736.

Useful Functions and Built-in Variables:

string_repeat
string_length
draw_text

Hints on Tackling This Assignment:

Set a variable to a random number, and format it with leading 0's.

GAMEMAKER PROGRAMMING CHALLENGES

Difficulty
2/5

20. Fading Moving Text

Project Outline:

Take a string and draw it moving and fading.

Useful Functions and Built-in Variables:

array_length
draw_set_*
draw_text_ext

Hints on Tackling This Assignment:

Place sentences in an array, and draw each in sequence that moves upwards and fades. When faded out, get next sentence and repeat.

21

21. Cool Down System

Difficulty 3/5

Project Outline:

Place a limit on how often a player can fire their weapon.

Useful Functions and Built-in Variables:

clamp
mouse_check_button_*
alarm

Hints on Tackling This Assignment:

Use a variable to determine whether a player can shoot or not, by increasing the value until it reaches a maximum. When max is reached, set a flag to prevent shooting and set an alarm. When alarm triggers allow shooting again.

GAMEMAKER PROGRAMMING CHALLENGES

Difficulty
2/5

22. Sliding Bar

Project Outline:

An adaptable system that allows the player to select a value by dragging a moving bar.

Useful Functions and Built-in Variables:

mouse_x
mouse_y
mouse_check_button_*
draw_sprite

Hints on Tackling This Assignment:

Detect if mouse button is pressed over a bar, if it is, move an indicator when mouse moves.

23. Variable Movement Speed

Difficulty 2/5

Project Outline:

A system that moves an instance to the mouse's position, slowing down as it gets closer.

Useful Functions and Built-in Variables:

`mouse_x`
`mouse_y`
`lerp`

Hints on Tackling This Assignment:

Use lerp to move an instance to the mouse's position, using a changing based on distance to the target, slowing down as it gets closer.

GAMEMAKER PROGRAMMING CHALLENGES

Difficulty
2/5

24. Rising Smoke Effect

Project Outline:

To use a sprite to make an interesting smoke rising effect.

Useful Functions and Built-in Variables:

motion_set
instance_destroy
draw_sprite_ext
mouse_check_button_pressed
instance_create_layer

Hints on Tackling This Assignment:

Create an instance that moves up and slowly fades out, that is then destroyed. Create using mouse_check_button_pressed and instance_create_layer.

Difficulty
2/5

25. Typewriter Text Effect

Project Outline:

Make a typewriter effect by drawing characters from a string one at time.

Useful Functions and Built-in Variables:

alarm
string_copy
string_length
draw_text

Hints on Tackling This Assignment:

Take one letter from a string and add it to another string, using an alarm to slowly do this. Display this string in a draw event.

GAMEMAKER PROGRAMMING CHALLENGES

Difficulty
3/5

26. Level Unlock System

Project Outline:

Create a visual system that shows the player which levels are currently locked / unlocked.

Useful Functions and Built-in Variables:

global
mouse_check_button_pressed
draw_sprite
draw_text

Hints on Tackling This Assignment:

Use a global value that can change on input from left and right mouse buttons. Use variable definitions to set values for different objects that draw differently depending on locked / unlocked status.

27. Weapon Management

Difficulty 4/5

Project Outline:

A system that allows the user to swap between different weapons, firing a different projectile for each. Allow user to purchase extra ammo.

Useful Functions and Built-in Variables:

global
draw_sprite
audio_play_sound
mouse_check_button
draw_text
instance_create_layer

Hints on Tackling This Assignment:

Use a 2D array to hold weapon data. If player has enough cash, allow user to buy extra ammon. Allow shooting of the weapon, create a basic object instance with a sprite assigned. Play appropriate sound for action.

28. Top Down Character Control

Project Outline:

Create a system with a character that can move in four directions, with a different sprite for each direction, and whether moving or not.

Useful Functions and Built-in Variables:

```
enum
keyboard_check
if
switch
```

Hints on Tackling This Assignment:

Set a sprite for each direction, and whether currently moving or not. Use variables to keep track. Draw appropriate sprite.

29. Blood Effect Using Particles

Difficulty 4/5

Project Outline:

A particle system to create a basic blood effect.

Useful Functions and Built-in Variables:

part_system_create
part_system_depth
part_system_destroy
part_type_*
part_particles_create

Hints on Tackling This Assignment:

Create a particle system by setting attributes. Display on screen at location of mouse when button is pressed.

GAMEMAKER PROGRAMMING CHALLENGES

Difficulty
2/5

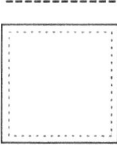

30. Draw Text Info With Background

Project Outline:

Make a basic system to show formatted text with a background. Set to destroy after 3 seconds.

Useful Functions and Built-in Variables:

draw_rectangle
draw_text
game_get_speed
alarm
draw_set_valign
draw_set_halign
draw_set_font

Hints on Tackling This Assignment:

Create a script that takes in a string and draws it centered over a rectangle. Set it to destroy after 3 seconds by setting an alarm.

31. Speed Boost

Difficulty 2/5

Project Outline:

Allow the player to temporary increase the max speed they can move at.

Useful Functions and Built-in Variables:

move_towards_point
mouse_x
mouse_y
draw_text
game_get_speed

Hints on Tackling This Assignment:

Use a true / false flag to determine if player currently has boost. On collision with an upgrade instance set flag to true and start alarm. On alarm reset flag. When flag is true, allow faster movement.

Difficulty 4/5

32. Projectile Curved Path

Project Outline:

A system to allow the player to create a projectile that follows a curved trajectory.

Useful Functions and Built-in Variables:

path_add
path_set_kind
path_add_point
path_start

Hints on Tackling This Assignment:

Add points on a path that the weapon follows. Set path to smooth using path_set_kind.

33. Draw Power Bar With Background

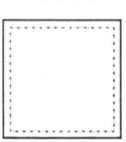

Project Outline:

Make a system that shows a value by drawing part of a sprite.

Useful Functions and Built-in Variables:

mouse_check_button
clamp
draw_rectangle

Hints on Tackling This Assignment:

Allow mouse buttons to change values. Draw background and draw a solid rectangle to cover up areas, reducing rectangle size to show the powerbar behind.

GAMEMAKER PROGRAMMING CHALLENGES

Difficulty
2/5

34. Create Muzzle Flash

Project Outline:

A weapon that can rotate and fire, creating a muzzle flash that is shown at the correct position and direction.

Useful Functions and Built-in Variables:

```
mouse_check_button
image_angle
instance_create_layer
lengthdir_*
```

Hints on Tackling This Assignment:

Allow player to rotate a turret. Create a muzzle flash, sending though the creator's id. Rotate flash to match creator's angle. Destroy muzzle flash when animation is finished.

Difficulty
1/5

35. Cloud Effect Using Effects

Project Outline:

Use GameMaker's effect layer to create a cloud effect.

Useful Functions and Built-in Variables:

No code.

Hints on Tackling This Assignment:

Create a cloud effect layer and set to something you like the look of.

GAMEMAKER PROGRAMMING CHALLENGES

Difficulty
2/5

36. Missile Smoke Trail

Project Outline:

Create a smoke effect trail for a moving projectile.

Useful Functions and Built-in Variables:

move_towards_point
point_direction
direction
image_angle
lengthdir_*
effect_create_layer

Hints on Tackling This Assignment:

Create an instance that moves towards the mouse's position, draw an effect at the rear of the instance, using lengthdir_*.

37. Selectable Stats

Difficulty 3/5

Project Outline:

Display a number of characters with different attributes that the player can choose from.

Useful Functions and Built-in Variables:

alarm
draw_rectangle
draw_line
for
draw_text

Hints on Tackling This Assignment:

Populate an array with data of sprite image and stats. Loop through using an alarm. Save to global values if current option is selected.

GAMEMAKER PROGRAMMING CHALLENGES

Difficulty
3/5

38. Add Playing Cards & Shuffle

Project Outline:

Use a suitable data structure to store playing cards, then shuffle and and select a card at random. Display the card as a sprite and text.

Useful Functions and Built-in Variables:

ds_list_*
sprite_get_name
real
string

Hints on Tackling This Assignment:

Add cards to a list or an array, shuffle the values and then choose the top card. Draw this sprite on screen with text detailing the card's suit and value.

39. Enemy Track Player's Movement

Difficulty 2/5

Project Outline:

To make an enemy that follows the player's movement on the y position.

Useful Functions and Built-in Variables:

mouse_y

Hints on Tackling This Assignment:

Move the enemy up or down to the player's y location.

Difficulty
3/5

40. Tool Tip Pop Up

Project Outline:

To draw an image and text when the mouse cursor is over an instance.

Useful Functions and Built-in Variables:

```
instance_position
draw_sprite
draw_text
draw_set_colour
```

Hints on Tackling This Assignment:

Detect if mouse is over an instance, if it is draw some data over a sprite bubble.

41. Pop-Up Wobbly Text

Difficulty 2/5

Project Outline:

To take a given string and draw it with a wobbling fading effect.

Useful Functions and Built-in Variables:

```
sin
draw_text_transformed
draw_set_alpha
```

Hints on Tackling This Assignment:

Use a sine wave to make the text Wobble by changing text angle. Change the y position and alpha to make it move up and fade.

42. Grow and Shrink Sprite Control

Project Outline:

Create a system that draws a sprite that grows, then shrinks, and is then destroyed.

Useful Functions and Built-in Variables:

image_xscale
image_yscale
game_get_speed
alarm

Hints on Tackling This Assignment:

Use a flag to determine if the sprite is growing or shrinking. Gradually change the scale of the sprite, from 0 and growing in size until an alarm triggers, then shrink back to 0 and destroy.

Difficulty
1/5

43. Smoothly Move To Mouse Position

Project Outline:

To move an instance to the mouse position.

Useful Functions and Built-in Variables:

mouse_x
mouse_y

Hints on Tackling This Assignment:

Move to the mouse cursor's position at a predefined speed.

Difficulty
1/5

44. Bounce Off Room Border

Project Outline:

To track the instances position, and change direction on collision with the room's border.

Useful Functions and Built-in Variables:

speed
direction
room_width
room_height

Hints on Tackling This Assignment:

Detect when a moving instance collides with a room border, and then make it change direction.

45. Pause Music When Sound Effect Plays

Difficulty 2/5

Project Outline:

Stop music from playing when a sound effect plays, then resume the music when the effect has finished playing.

Useful Functions and Built-in Variables:

audio_play_sound
audio_pause_sound
audio_is_playing
audio_resume_sound

Hints on Tackling This Assignment:

Create a variable and set playing sound to it. If sound effect plays, pause the music and resume when effect has finished.

GAMEMAKER PROGRAMMING CHALLENGES

Difficulty
3/5

46. Glitch Effect Text

Project Outline:

To make some text shake and change colour.

Useful Functions and Built-in Variables:

irandom_range
draw_set_color
draw_set_font
draw_text
choose

Hints on Tackling This Assignment:

Draw text with some randomness of its position. Use another random value to change the drawing colour.

47. Wobbly Text

Difficulty 2/5

Project Outline:

Take each letter of a string and make it move up and down using a sine wave.

Useful Functions and Built-in Variables:

string_length
for
draw_text
sin

Hints on Tackling This Assignment:

Get letters from a string and draw them with changing y values so the letters have a wave effect.

Difficulty
1/5

48. Choose A Random Instance

Project Outline:

To count all instances and then choose one at random.

Useful Functions and Built-in Variables:

```
instance_exists
instance_number
move_towards_point
distance_to_point
instance_find
irandom
```

Hints on Tackling This Assignment:

Make an instance that randomly targets another instance using instance_find. Move towards the target and stop when reached.

49. Draw Mini Healthbar

Difficulty 2/5

Project Outline:

Use GameMaker's built function that draws the enemy's hp that follows the instance as it moves.

Useful Functions and Built-in Variables:

```
clamp
sprite_width
sprite_height
draw_healthbar
```

Hints on Tackling This Assignment:

Draw the healthbar relative to the sprite origin. Base barsize on current hp and starting value.

50. Fade In And Out

Difficulty 2/5

Project Outline:

To gradually change the alpha of a sprite so it fades in and out.

Useful Functions and Built-in Variables:

```
draw_sprite_ext
if
else
```

Hints on Tackling This Assignment:

Use a flag to determine if the instance is fading in or out. Change a variable between 0 and 1, and back to 0, using this value for the sprite's alpha value.

51. Rotating Text

Difficulty 2/5

Project Outline:

Take a string and rotate it around its center.

Useful Functions and Built-in Variables:

draw_set_font
string_width
lengthdir_*
draw_text_transformed

Hints on Tackling This Assignment:

Calculate the width of a string and use that value with angle and lengthdir_* functions to set the rotation point.

GAMEMAKER PROGRAMMING CHALLENGES

Difficulty
2/5

52. Flashing Text

Project Outline:

Take some text and draw it so it flashes.

Useful Functions and Built-in Variables:

make_colour_rgb
current_time
random
draw_set_color
draw_text

Hints on Tackling This Assignment:

Set a variable to a colour using random and current_time.

Difficulty
2/5

53. Play Sound At Selected Volume

Project Outline:

To play sound at different volume, depending on user input.

Useful Functions and Built-in Variables:

```
mouse_check_button
audio_play_sound
```

Hints on Tackling This Assignment:

Set an attribute for audio_play_sound that plays at a different volume based on player input.

GAMEMAKER PROGRAMMING CHALLENGES

Difficulty
2/5

54. Spawn Power-Ups System

Project Outline:

To spawn different powerups at random, weighted according to upgrade type.

Useful Functions and Built-in Variables:

floor
random
if
else

Hints on Tackling This Assignment:

Create a random value, and check with a range of values to decide what to do. For example, choose a random number between 0 and 100. If between 1 and 10, upgrade player's weapon.

Difficulty 2/5

55. Move Crosshair To Mouse Position

Project Outline:

To make a system that moves a crosshair to the mouse's position, that stops when target is reached.

Useful Functions and Built-in Variables:

mouse_x
mouse_y
distance_to_point
move_towards_point
speed

Hints on Tackling This Assignment:

Set a target as the current mouse position using move_towards_point to move towards it, when close stop movement by setting speed to 0.

56. Checkpoint System

Difficulty 3/5

Project Outline:

To store the player's last collision with a checkpoint, and move to that position when the player dies.

Useful Functions and Built-in Variables:

mouse_check_button_pressed
x
y

Hints on Tackling This Assignment:

Save the player's position to variables when colliding with a checkpoint. Upon mouse click move to stored position.

Difficulty
3/5

57. Check If Instance Is In View

Project Outline:

Write a script that takes an instance's position and returns whether it is within the current view.

Useful Functions and Built-in Variables:

camera_get_view_x
camera_get_view_y
camera_get_view_width
camera_get_view_height
point_in_rectangle

Hints on Tackling This Assignment:

Send the instances x and x position to a script that check if those values are within the view, and returns true or false.

GAMEMAKER PROGRAMMING CHALLENGES

Difficulty
5/5

58. Jump Through Platforms

Project Outline:

To create a one-way platform that the player can jump through from below.

Useful Functions and Built-in Variables:

gravity
bbox_bottom
bbox_top
vspeed

Hints on Tackling This Assignment:

Check if player is currently jumping within a crate, if it is allow jumping again.

Difficulty 1/5

59. Random Level Music

Project Outline:

Choose random music, from a selection of tracks.

Useful Functions and Built-in Variables:

choose
audio_play_sound

Hints on Tackling This Assignment:

Use choose to select a random track, and audio_play_sound to play it.

GAMEMAKER PROGRAMMING CHALLENGES

Difficulty
3/5

60. Exploding Effect

Project Outline:

Split a sprite into multiple parts to create an exploding effect.

Useful Functions and Built-in Variables:

sprite_get_number
for
instance_create_layer
direction

Hints on Tackling This Assignment:

Use a sprite editor to break a sprite into sections. Count the number of sprites and send each flying in a different direction with help of a for loop. A useful tool: https://www.gamedeveloperstudio.com/tools/spritesheet_slicer.php

61

Difficulty
2/5

61. Draw Text With Border

Project Outline:

Make a script that takes in text and position to draw text with a border.

Useful Functions and Built-in Variables:

draw_text
draw_set_colour

Hints on Tackling This Assignment:

Create a script that takes in a string, colours and position. Draw at position with some variance in position to make a border, then draw text again over it.

GAMEMAKER PROGRAMMING CHALLENGES

Difficulty
3/5

62. Move Coin To Score Text

Project Outline:

Make an object spawn and move to the position of the players score.

Useful Functions and Built-in Variables:

`move_towards_point`
`distance_to_point`

Hints on Tackling This Assignment:

Spawn a coin and make it fade by changing the alpha value. Move to the position where the score is drawn, increase score and destroy when target position is reached.

63. Tire Track Effects

Project Outline:

To draw tyre tracks that fade away, taking into account the direction of the vehicle.

Useful Functions and Built-in Variables:

lengthdir_*
image_angle
alarm
instance_create_layer
draw_sprite_ext

Hints on Tackling This Assignment:

Use an alarm to create an instance of a tyre track, pass through angle to use. Use lengthdir_* to set correct position. Fade out tyre and destroy when done.

Difficulty 3/5

Difficulty
1/5

64. Fireworks Display

Project Outline:

Use GameMaker's built-in effects to create a colourful fireworks display.

Useful Functions and Built-in Variables:

```
random_range
irandom
choose
effect_create_layer
```

Hints on Tackling This Assignment:

Choose a random position in the room, a random size, and random colour. Draw this using effect_create_layer.

65. Spawn Bullets From Double Weapon

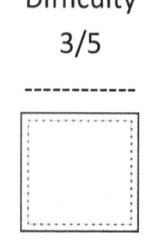

Difficulty
3/5

Project Outline:

To spawn multiple projectiles at the correct location, taking into account the rotation of the weapon.

Useful Functions and Built-in Variables:

lengthdir_*
image_angle
instance_create_layer

Hints on Tackling This Assignment:

Use lengthdir_* recursively to spawn two bullets at the barrels of a double weapon. Send through direction and angle when creating the bullets.

**Difficulty
2/5**

66. Sprite Drop Shadow

Project Outline:

Use the instances sprite to create a simple drop shadow.

Useful Functions and Built-in Variables:

draw_sprite_ext
draw_sprite

Hints on Tackling This Assignment:

Draw the shadow by drawing with draw_sprite_ext setting colour to black and a partial alpha, at an offset. Draw main sprite above.

67. Simple Top Down Collision

Difficulty 3/5

Project Outline:

Create a collision that detects if a crate is to the left or right, if so prevent movement.

Useful Functions and Built-in Variables:

mouse_check_button
lengthdir_*
hspeed
point_direction
other
speed

Hints on Tackling This Assignment:

Move the player with mouse buttons. Stop movement if colliding with a crate, moving the crate a small distance upon collision.

68. Spawn Instance With Random Subimage

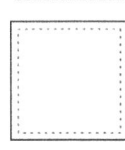

Project Outline:

Make a system that spawns an instance every 4 seconds. When spawned instances drop from the top of room to the bottom.

Useful Functions and Built-in Variables:

instance_create_layer
alarm
image_number
irandom
random_range
image_speed

Hints on Tackling This Assignment:

Use an alarm to spawn instances above the room. Select a random subimage using irandom and set a vertical speed. Use image_speed to prevent animation.

69. Sine Wave Based Movement

Difficulty 2/5

Project Outline:

Use a sine wave to make an instance move slowly up and down.

Useful Functions and Built-in Variables:
```
sin
current_time
```

Hints on Tackling This Assignment:

Use a sine wave based on current_time to move an instance up and down.

GAMEMAKER PROGRAMMING CHALLENGES

Difficulty
3/5

70. Draw Player's Speed On Dial

Project Outline:

To make a dial with a rotating pin that shows the player's movement speed.

Useful Functions and Built-in Variables:

clamp
mouse_check_button
draw_sprite_ext

Hints on Tackling This Assignment:

Allow mouse buttons to increase / decrease a speed value within a range using clamp. Convert the speed into an angle to draw a pin over a dial.

71. Spawn Trees Border

Difficulty 2/5

Project Outline:

To create system that automatically spawns trees on the left and right sides of a room, incorporating some randomness.

Useful Functions and Built-in Variables:

```
room_height
room_width
for
instance_create_layer
```

Hints on Tackling This Assignment:

Calculate how many trees by dividing room height by gap distance. Use a for loop to place at edges of room, with a little randomness.

72. One Button Controlled Movement

Project Outline:

Allow the player to move a crosshair around the room using just a single mouse button as input.

Useful Functions and Built-in Variables:

mouse_check_button
motion_set
clamp

Hints on Tackling This Assignment:

Rotate an indicator around a crosshair. If mouse button is down, move crosshair in the indicators direction. Use clamp to keep instance within the room.

73. Plane Movement

Difficulty 3/5

Project Outline:

Create a player object that can move up and down using a single mouse button as input. Change the sprite's angle to match direction.

Useful Functions and Built-in Variables:

mouse_check_button
clamp
image_angle
direction

Hints on Tackling This Assignment:

Change flying angle based on mouse button down or not. Change image_angle to match direction. Use clamp to keep in room and limit turning angle.

GAMEMAKER PROGRAMMING CHALLENGES

Difficulty
3/5

74. Player Power Up Creator

Project Outline:

Make a system that requires a player to mash a button in order to receive a power up.

Useful Functions and Built-in Variables:

mouse_check_button_*
clamp

Hints on Tackling This Assignment:

Increase a value each time left or right mouse button is tapped. Reduce value each frame. If target is reached, set a flag to true and display "Target Reached".

75. Coin Drop Bonus Effect

Difficulty 2/5

Project Outline:

Spawn coins that fall from the top of the room, which then explode and create a graphical effect.

Useful Functions and Built-in Variables:

irandom_range
vspeed
random_range
effect_create_layer

Hints on Tackling This Assignment:

Spawn an instance above room y, set a random x position, set a random falling vspeed and random distance to travel before exploding. Create effect when distance reached, and destroy.

Difficulty
3/5

76. Endless Levels

Project Outline:

Create an endless level by using a fixed view, and have instances move across the screen.

Useful Functions and Built-in Variables:

sprite_index
choose
vspeed
room_height
sprite_height

Hints on Tackling This Assignment:

Use an alarm to spawn instances above the room that movedown. Repeat to give the appearance of an endless level.

Difficulty
3/5

77. Mini Healthbar With Segments

Project Outline:

To draw a healthbar and overlay it with lines to create segments.

Useful Functions and Built-in Variables:

```
clamp
draw_healthbar
draw_line
```

Hints on Tackling This Assignment:

Draw a healthbar with current hp. Draw vertical lines over the bar.

Difficulty
5/5

78. Outline Shader

Project Outline:

Use a basic shader to draw an outline around any given sprite.

Useful Functions and Built-in Variables:

shader_get_uniform
shader_set_uniform_f

Hints on Tackling This Assignment:

An example of setting a shader to adjust a sprite image. Just an example of how to apply a shader. If you are new to shaders, see: `https://learnopengl.com/`

79. Move Crosshair To Target

Project Outline:

Make a system that chooses a random enemy and moves towards it. On mouse click destroy it and seek out a new target.

Useful Functions and Built-in Variables:

```
clamp
place_meeting
with
move_towards_point
```

Hints on Tackling This Assignment:

If one or more instances exist, choose one to target. Move crosshair to target. When over it change crosshair sprite. Shoot with mouse button to kill and select new target.

80. Spawn Items With Gap

Difficulty 3/5

Project Outline:

To make a system that randomly spawns instances, which then move apart.

Useful Functions and Built-in Variables:

```
ds_list_size
lengthdir_*
for
with
collision_circle_list
```

Hints on Tackling This Assignment:

Spawn instances at random positions in room. Use collision_circle_list to check instances within range. Loop through these and move them away.

81. Add Scores To A List

Difficulty 2/5

Project Outline:

To create a system that remembers the players last 10 scores and displays on screen, updating and culling as new scores are added.

Useful Functions and Built-in Variables:

ds_list_create
ds_list_delete
ds_list_size
for
draw_text

Hints on Tackling This Assignment:

Add values to a ds_list. culling oldest entry when above a certain length. Use a for loop to position and draw values from the array.

GAMEMAKER PROGRAMMING CHALLENGES

Difficulty
2/5

82. Cloud Effect

Project Outline:

Use layers to draw clouds both in front and behind a player.

Useful Functions and Built-in Variables:

image_index
choose
sprite_width
room_width

Hints on Tackling This Assignment:

Place a number of cloud objects on layers behind and infront of the player's layer. Set to move at random speed / direction. Wrap round the room.

83. Ball Bouncing Off Instances

Difficulty 2/5

Project Outline:

To create a simple system that makes a ball bounce off of wall instances.

Useful Functions and Built-in Variables:

motion_set
choose
move_bounce_all

Hints on Tackling This Assignment:

Set in motion with motion_set. Make the ball bounce off of instances with move_bounce_all.

GAMEMAKER PROGRAMMING CHALLENGES

Difficulty
1/5

84. Keeping A Value In A Range

Project Outline:

To keep a variable within a range of two other values.

Useful Functions and Built-in Variables:

clamp
mouse_check_button

Hints on Tackling This Assignment:

Use two variables, one for min value and one for max.
Use clamp to keep a value in a range between them.
Allow mouse buttons to change value.

Difficulty 4/5

85. Film Style Scrolling Credits

Project Outline:

To add text values to an array and display them moving up the screen whilst shrinking.

Useful Functions and Built-in Variables:

array_length
alarm
room_height
array_delete
instance_create_layer
draw_text_ext_transformed

Hints on Tackling This Assignment:

Create an array to hold sentences. Take top entry when an alarm triggers and send through to a drawing instance. Repeat until all text is shown.

GAMEMAKER PROGRAMMING CHALLENGES

Difficulty
2/5

86. Rotate Room View

Project Outline:

Allow player to rotate the view, within a given range.

Useful Functions and Built-in Variables:

camera_set_view_angle
clamp
mouse_check_button

Hints on Tackling This Assignment:

Create a variable for the angle, change with mouse buttons, and use clamp to keep in range. Use the camera function to set this angle.

Difficulty
2/5

87. Toggle Full Screen

Project Outline:

Allow user to toggle between full screen and windowed. Do this by setting window_set_fullscreen to true or false.

Useful Functions and Built-in Variables:

```
window_set_fullscreen
keyboard_check
```

Hints on Tackling This Assignment:

Allow a keypress to toggle a value between true and false. Use this flag to set as full screen or not.

Difficulty
3/5

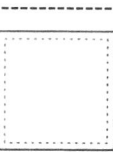

88. Progress Bar

Project Outline:

Draw a bar that indicates the player's current level progress.

Useful Functions and Built-in Variables:

draw_healthbar
for
draw_line
room_width
room_height

Hints on Tackling This Assignment:

Calculate level progress as a percentage. Use this value to draw a healthbar. Use lines to draw segments.

Difficulty
3/5

89. Flash Player To Show Damage

Project Outline:

Make the player's sprite temporarily red to indicate that it has received some damage.

Useful Functions and Built-in Variables:

alarm
draw_sprite_ext
draw_sprite

Hints on Tackling This Assignment:

Use a flag to determine if player currently has damage. Use an alarm to reset flag. Draw with red colour if damaged, else draw normally.

90. Fade Between Two Images

Project Outline:

Fade between two subimages to create a graphical effect.

Useful Functions and Built-in Variables:

enum
draw_sprite_ext
if

Hints on Tackling This Assignment:

Use a variable that slowly toggles between 0 and 1, using a state machine. Draw an image at this alpha value, and another at 1-this value.

91. Draw A Path As Circles

Difficulty 4/5

Project Outline:

Devise a method to draw equally spaced circles along a path.

Useful Functions and Built-in Variables:

path_get_length
draw_circle
path_get_x
path_get_y

Hints on Tackling This Assignment:

Get length of a path, use this to position and draw circles at regular positions along this path.

Difficulty
2/5

92. Simple Top Down Control

Project Outline:

To create a system that allows a player to move in a top down game using only a single mouse button input.

Useful Functions and Built-in Variables:

clamp
mouse_check_button
image_angle
direction

Hints on Tackling This Assignment:

Use a variable for rotating that increases or decreasing depending on if button is down or not. Move and face direction of travel. Keep in room using clamp.

Difficulty
3/5

93. Laser To Target

Project Outline:

To draw a laser to the mouse's x position, using drawing functions.

Useful Functions and Built-in Variables:

draw_line
draw_circle
mouse_x

Hints on Tackling This Assignment:

Draw a horizontal line from weapon tip to mouse's x position. Draw a red circle at laser tip.

GAMEMAKER PROGRAMMING CHALLENGES

Difficulty
3/5

94. Bubble Explosion Effect

Project Outline:

Create a bubble explosion of multiple bubbles that rise up and pop.

Useful Functions and Built-in Variables:

```
choose
alarm
audio_play_sound
instance_create_layer
repeat
```

Hints on Tackling This Assignment:

Spawn bubbles that move out in random direction and speed. Add some negative gravity to make them float. Destroy with an alarm and play a random sound.

95. Grid Movement Control

Difficulty 4/5

Project Outline:

Create grid that blocks out areas where boxes are located, move from start to end point whilst avoiding the boxes.

Useful Functions and Built-in Variables:

mp_grid_create
mp_grid_add_instances
mp_grid_path
path_set_kind
path_start

Hints on Tackling This Assignment:

Make a maze of boxes. Make instance navigate the path between start and end points, whilst avoiding the boxes. Use an mp_grid_path for this.

Difficulty
3/5

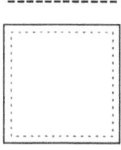

96. Image Scale, Fade and Rotate Effect

Project Outline:

To create an instance that rotates, grows in size and fades out.

Useful Functions and Built-in Variables:

choose
draw_sprite_ext

Hints on Tackling This Assignment:

Choose a random direction to rotate. Slowly increase in size and fade out. Use draw_sprite_ext to set size and fade out.

Difficulty 2/5

97. Player Streak

Project Outline:

Keep track of a player's streak count and display on screen.

Useful Functions and Built-in Variables:

draw_text
draw_set_font

Hints on Tackling This Assignment:

Increase a variable every time something happens. Reset when something else happens, for example hitting an enemy bullet. Draw this value onscreen.

GAMEMAKER PROGRAMMING CHALLENGES

Difficulty
5/5

98. Numbers As Text

Project Outline:

Convert numbers to text, for example 16783 to sixteen thousand seven hundred and eighty three.

Useful Functions and Built-in Variables:

div
mod
switch
break
return

Hints on Tackling This Assignment:

Set a variable to a random value up to 100,000. Use a look-up table and logic to convert in text. This will be easier if start at units, tens, hundreds, then thousands.

99. Draw Lives As Images

Difficulty 1/5

Project Outline:

To take the player's current number of lives and draw on screen using sprites.

Useful Functions and Built-in Variables:

```
lives
clamp
for
draw_sprite
```

Hints on Tackling This Assignment:

Loop through a for loop for the number of lives. Use draw_sprite to draw them, using values of loop to set position of each sprite. Use clamp to keep within a range.

Difficulty
3/5

100. Coin Explosion Effect

Project Outline:

To make a coin explosion effect that shoots out coins in multiple directions.

Useful Functions and Built-in Variables:

for
instance_create_layer
direction
speed

Hints on Tackling This Assignment:

Use a for loop that loops through and creates coins that uses the loop value to move coins in different directions.

Difficulty
2/5

101. Follow Object

Project Outline:

Make a system where one instance can follow another whilst remaining at a distance.

Useful Functions and Built-in Variables:

instance_exists
distance_to_object
move_towards_point
speed
point_direction

Hints on Tackling This Assignment:

Move towards a player until a certain distance away using distance_to_object, and set speed to 0 when close. Make it point towards direction of travel.

102. Orbit Object

Difficulty 3/5

Project Outline:

Make one instance orbit around another, updating if the target instance moves position.

Useful Functions and Built-in Variables:

lengthdir_*
mod

Hints on Tackling This Assignment:

Increase a variable for the angle, using mod to keep in range. Use lengthdir_* to rotate it around a player.

GAMEMAKER PROGRAMMING CHALLENGES

Difficulty
3/5

103. Random Name Generator

Project Outline:

Use a random collection of short strings to generate a unique name for a game character.

Useful Functions and Built-in Variables:

choose
draw_text

Hints on Tackling This Assignment:

Choose a selection of name parts at random using choose function. Combine these together to make a name and draw on screen.

Difficulty 3/5

104. Top Down Movement

Project Outline:

Allow player to move in four directions, preventing movement if a crate is in the way.

Useful Functions and Built-in Variables:

`keyboard_check`
`place_meeting`

Hints on Tackling This Assignment:

Move the player with keyboard WSAD. Only allow movement if no crate in direction of travel.

105. Screen Shake

Difficulty 2/5

Project Outline:

Shake the current view randomly when a flag is set to true, both in position and angle.

Useful Functions and Built-in Variables:

```
camera_get_view_*
camera_set_view_pos
camera_set_view_angle
irandom_range
```

Hints on Tackling This Assignment:

Use a flag to set if a shake is current or not. When started set max count. Randomly change view position and angle until count reached. Then reset.

106. Bomb Destruction Zone

Project Outline:

To give damage to wide area by creating multiple explosive instances.

Useful Functions and Built-in Variables:

```
call_later
instance_create_layer
mouse_check_button_*
mouse_x
mouse_y
```

Hints on Tackling This Assignment:

Upon mouse button, create a bomb. Then use call_later to set a timer to create other explosions that radiate outwards.

107. Circular Healthbar

Difficulty 4/5

Project Outline:

Draw health as a circular bar that takes into account theinstances current hp.

Useful Functions and Built-in Variables:

clamp
lengthdir_*
draw_set_colour
draw_line_width
for

Hints on Tackling This Assignment:

Loop 360 degrees using a for loop. Then use lengthdir_* functions to set start and end points to draw a series of lines. Set colour depending on the health value.

108. Volume Based On Distance

Difficulty 3/5

Project Outline:

Calculate the distance between two instances, and base the volume of a sound on this value.

Useful Functions and Built-in Variables:

```
audio_play_sound
distance_to_object
audio_sound_gain
clamp
```

Hints on Tackling This Assignment:

Start playing a sound and assign to a variable. Use distance between two points to set volume between 0 and 1. Use audio_sound_gain to adjust the volume.

Difficulty
1/5

109. Snow Weather Effect

Project Outline:

Use GameMaker's built-in effects to create some snow.

Useful Functions and Built-in Variables:

effect_create_layer
ef_snow

Hints on Tackling This Assignment:

Just call effect_create_layer and use ef_snow.
Call this within a step event.

GAMEMAKER PROGRAMMING CHALLENGES

Difficulty
3/5

110. Password Easter Egg

Project Outline:

Unlock secret features if the player types in a secret code.

Useful Functions and Built-in Variables:

keyboard_check_pressed
keyboard_string
if

Hints on Tackling This Assignment:

Set a variable string to the password. Use keyboard string to compare to password, if true change a flag. Use space to clear keyboard_string.

111

111. Average Position Between 2 Instances

Difficulty 2/5

Project Outline:

To get the location that is halfway between two instances.

Useful Functions and Built-in Variables:

draw_circle
x
y

Hints on Tackling This Assignment:

Get the origin of two instances, calculate a midway point for the x and y positions. Draw a circle at that position.

112. Random Dice Rolls

Project Outline:

To randomly roll 2 six-sided dice, show them visually and calculate the total.

Useful Functions and Built-in Variables:

enum
mouse_check_button
draw_sprite
irandom
draw_text

Hints on Tackling This Assignment:

When player clicks left button show values of two random dice for 4 seconds by showing random subimages. After time stop rolling and show dice as images and text showing total value.

Difficulty
4/5

113. On Screen Keyboard

Project Outline:

Create an on-screen keyboard, which the user can click with a mouse button to enter text.

Useful Functions and Built-in Variables:

image_index
mouse_check_button
instance_position
mouse_check_button_*

Hints on Tackling This Assignment:

Place buttons in the room laid out like a keyboard. When clicked add their letter to a string. Allow enter to set string, delete to reset.

Difficulty
2/5

114. Ds List Sort

Project Outline:

To take (n) words and sort them alphabetically in ascending or descending order.

Useful Functions and Built-in Variables:

mouse_check_button_*
ds_list_create
ds_list_add
ds_list_sort
ds_list_size

Hints on Tackling This Assignment:

Populate an array with strings. Draw entries on screen. Left and right mouse buttons to sort ascending or descending, using ds_list_sort.

Difficulty
3/5

115. Colour Picker

Project Outline:

Display a colour wheel, and allow the user to click and select any colour. Use this value to display some text.

Useful Functions and Built-in Variables:

draw_set_colour
draw_getpixel
mouse_check_button

Hints on Tackling This Assignment:

Draw a colour wheel sprite. Allow clicking to save a colour. Draw text in saved colour.

116. Numbers To Speech

Project Outline:

Create a system that converts a number variable into speech, using a separate sound for each element.

Useful Functions and Built-in Variables:

ds_list_size
audio_is_playing
audio_play_sound
ds_list_delete

Hints on Tackling This Assignment:

Break down a random number into parts and queue each part in a list. Loop through the list and play each audio part. Record your audio, or see download resources for this book.

Difficulty 3/5

117. Teleport

Project Outline:

Create an object that when a player collides with it they are transported to another set position within the room

Useful Functions and Built-in Variables:

instance_place
keyboard_check

Hints on Tackling This Assignment:

Move the player with WSAD. When a player collides with a teleport item, change position to near new target (not touching to prevent an infinite loop).

118. Queued Messages

Difficulty
3/5

Project Outline:

To store a series of messages, and display them in sequence.

Useful Functions and Built-in Variables:

ds_list_create
ds_list_add
alarm

Hints on Tackling This Assignment:

Create a ds_list holding strings to display. Grab top entry and save to variable, delete entry. Draw the variable on screen. Repeat until list is empty.

119. Shop System

Difficulty
13/5

Project Outline:

To create a system that allows a player to buy items (if they have enough money), along with the ability to sell them.

Useful Functions and Built-in Variables:

```
position_meeting
mouse_check_button
```

Hints on Tackling This Assignment:

Populate a 2D array with data: sprite, name, amount, cost and selling price. Create buttons to buy if enough cash. And to sell. Update data after transaction.

Difficulty
3/5

120. Parallax Background

Project Outline:

Create a parallax effect by using multiple background layers.

Useful Functions and Built-in Variables:

layer_get_id
layer_y
keyboard_check
clamp

Hints on Tackling This Assignment:

Set a layered backgrounds that move at different horizontal speeds. Allow WS to move layers up and down. Use clamp to keep y position within a range.

121. Eight Directional Movement A

Difficulty 3/5

Project Outline:

Allow the player to move in 8 directions using a combination of key-presses. Use a different sprite for each direction.

Useful Functions and Built-in Variables:

keyboard_check
lengthdir_*
sprite_index
image_speed

Hints on Tackling This Assignment:

Allow WSAD to move a character in 8 directions. Use a different sprite for each direction and only animate when moving. Use lengthdir_* to apply movement.

122. Room Transition Fade In & Out

Difficulty 3/5

Project Outline:

Create an effect that fades in on room start, and fades out when moving to a different room.

Useful Functions and Built-in Variables:

draw_set_alpha
draw_rectangle
draw_set_colour

Hints on Tackling This Assignment:

Draw a black rectangle over the room with changing alpha. Make something happen when fade out is complete.

Difficulty
2/5

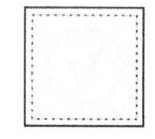

123. Nine Slice Example

Project Outline:

Use nine-slice to draw boxes with borders, that can be resized within the room.

Useful Functions and Built-in Variables:

draw_sprite_ext

Hints on Tackling This Assignment:

Set a sprite for nine-slice. Use draw_sprite_ext's image scale setting to set the size of the rectangle.

124. Hit Box A

Project Outline:

Create a collision instance when a player attacks, which can be used to detect a collision with an enemy.

Useful Functions and Built-in Variables:

alarm
image_speed
instance_destroy
mouse_check_button_*
instance_create_layer
image_index

Hints on Tackling This Assignment:

When player attacks, change its sprite animation, and on a certain frame create an instance that can be used to detect hits on an enemy.

GAMEMAKER PROGRAMMING CHALLENGES

Difficulty
1/5

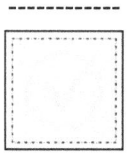

125. Snap To Grid

Project Outline:

Allow the user to place instances of a weapon base in the room, which snap to a grid position.

Useful Functions and Built-in Variables:

move_snap
mouse_x
mouse_y
mouse_check_button_*
instance_create_layer

Hints on Tackling This Assignment:

Move an instance with mouse, using move_snap to position it. Allow mouse button to create an instance at the position.

Difficulty
3/5

126. Hide & Seek

Project Outline:

Create a detection system that makes an enemy move towards the player if it can see it.

Useful Functions and Built-in Variables:

```
collision_line
move_towards_point
speed
draw_line
```

Hints on Tackling This Assignment:

Use a flag to determine if enemy can see player.
If true, move towards the player. If false stop moving.

Difficulty 2/5

127. Save Highscore

Project Outline:

To create a system that saves and loads a player's highscore.

Useful Functions and Built-in Variables:

```
ini_open
ini_close
ini_read_real
ini_write_real
mouse_check_button_*
```

Hints on Tackling This Assignment:

Load any saved score from an ini file. Create a random score value, if higher than saved score, save to the ini file.

128. Sprite Animation Control

Difficulty 3/5

Project Outline:

Create a simple system to play an animation and then return to idle when animation is complete.

Useful Functions and Built-in Variables:

keyboard_check_pressed
image_index
image_speed
image_number

Hints on Tackling This Assignment:

Allow player to press keys to change sprite index and set image index as 0. After animation is completed, change to idle sprite, checking with image_number.

GAMEMAKER PROGRAMMING CHALLENGES

Difficulty
2/5

129. Jet Pack & Gravity

Project Outline:

Allow player to fly up when a mouse button, slowly move down if not pressed.

Useful Functions and Built-in Variables:

gravity
image_angle
mouse_check_button
motion_add
clamp

Hints on Tackling This Assignment:

Set gravity of the player. If mouse button is down, add motion. Use clamp to keep in room.

130. Enemy Movement On Platform

Project Outline:

Create an enemy that automatically changes direction when it reaches the end of a platform.

Useful Functions and Built-in Variables:

sign
instance_position
image_xscale

Hints on Tackling This Assignment:

Check for no platform ahead of player in direction of movement using sign and instance_position. Use image_xscale to point in direction of movement.

**Difficulty
1/5**

131. Tweening

Project Outline:

To slowly move an instance between two points with speed based on the distance remaining.

Useful Functions and Built-in Variables:

```
lerp
enum
```

Hints on Tackling This Assignment:

Set up a start and end point. Move between the two points using lerp. Use enum for a basic state machine to manage directions.

Difficulty 2/5

132. Door & Key

Project Outline:

Create a system that only allows a player to open a door when they have the correct key.

Useful Functions and Built-in Variables:

xprevious
yprevious
keyboard_check
instance_destroy

Hints on Tackling This Assignment:

Use a flag to set whether player has a key or not. Set true if player collects the key. Destroy door on collision if true. Use *previous to move away from door if false.

Difficulty
1/5

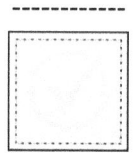

133. Wrap Instance Around Room

Project Outline:

Create a system that wraps around the room when they pass the room's borders. Draw on both edges when wrapping.

Useful Functions and Built-in Variables:

draw_sprite
clamp
room_width
sprite_width

Hints on Tackling This Assignment:

Detect when a sprite of an instance is overlapping a border. If it is draw the overlapping part on other border.

134. Change Transparency On Collision

Difficulty 2/5

Project Outline:

Make a system that changes an instance's image alpha when it collides with the player.

Useful Functions and Built-in Variables:

place_meeting
draw_sprite_ext

Hints on Tackling This Assignment:

Use a variable for setting an alpha value. Upon collision with an instanceor not, change this value.

Difficulty 2/5

135. Weapon Upgrade System

Project Outline:

Create a system that allows upgrading and downgrading of a weapon, creating a different missile based on the weapon.

Useful Functions and Built-in Variables:

```
image_number
alarm
keyboard_check_pressed
clamp
instance_create_layer
```

Hints on Tackling This Assignment:

Allow keys to change current weapon. Use an alarm to spawn projectiles, type of which depends on current weapon.

136. Knockback

Difficulty 3/5

Project Outline:

To create a knockback system where a player is pushed back a certain direction, then continues moving as normal.

Useful Functions and Built-in Variables:

```
mouse_check_button_*
alarm
else
```

Hints on Tackling This Assignment:

Set an alarm and flag when left button pressed. When flag is true move backwards. When alarm triggers, change flag and move forward.

137. Road Builder

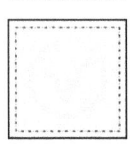

Difficulty
3/5

Project Outline:

Allow the user to place blocks next to currently placed instances.

Useful Functions and Built-in Variables:

place_meeting
mouse_check_button_*
instance_create_layer

Hints on Tackling This Assignment:

Snap the cursor to block size. Only allow placement if next to an existing block piece, by checking positions up, down, left, and right of current position.

GAMEMAKER PROGRAMMING CHALLENGES

Difficulty
3/5

138. Select Multiple Troops

Project Outline:

Allow player to click and drag to create an area, then select and store id of all these instances.

Useful Functions and Built-in Variables:

draw_rectangle
bbox_*
ds_list_create
collision_rectangle
ds_list_clear

Hints on Tackling This Assignment:

Allow player to click and drag to draw rectangle. Use collision_rectangle to get id's of all instances within it. Draw which instances have been selected.

Difficulty 3/5

139. Road Connections

Project Outline:

Allow player to click and add road parts, setting the correct sprite to make them connect.

Useful Functions and Built-in Variables:

```
position_meeting
instance_create_layer
floor
```

Hints on Tackling This Assignment:

Allow player to click / drag to place road instances.
Change road sprite depending on neighbors so road connects.

140. Lightning Effect

Project Outline:

Draw a lightning effect between a position and the mouse cursor, with some randomness with the paths of lines.

Useful Functions and Built-in Variables:

```
point_direction
point_distance
lengthdir_*
random
draw_line
do
until
```

Hints on Tackling This Assignment:

Use draw_line to draw lines between two points. Use random to set direction to create a lightning effect.

Difficulty
2/5

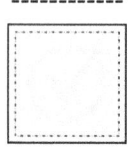

141. Gravity Movement

Project Outline:

Create some instances with different amounts of gravity.

Useful Functions and Built-in Variables:

gravity
vspeed
position_meeting

Hints on Tackling This Assignment:

Create 3 objects with different gravity. Move upwards when clicked, by setting a negative vspeed. Stop when colliding with an obstacle.

GAMEMAKER PROGRAMMING CHALLENGES

Difficulty
3/5

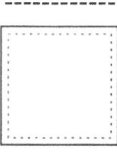

142. Blood Damage Effect

Project Outline:

Create a blood effect from sprites, that drips down and fades.

Useful Functions and Built-in Variables:

image_index
image_speed
image_angle
alarm
draw_sprite_ext

Hints on Tackling This Assignment:

Upon mouse click spawn a number of blood instances with random subimage and angle, that move down screen. Set an alarm that when triggered stops the blood moving and fades it.

143. Tap Instance To Change Image

Difficulty 1/5

Project Outline:

To create an instance that changes it's subimage when tapped.

Useful Functions and Built-in Variables:

```
mouse_check_button_*
image_number
draw_sprite
```

Hints on Tackling This Assignment:

Use a value that increase when the sprite is tapped with mouseclick. Draw the appropriate subimage.

144. Bullet Holes

Project Outline:

Place a bullet hole effect at the location a player shoots at, disappearing after a small amount of time.

Useful Functions and Built-in Variables:

irandom
alarm
instance_destroy

Hints on Tackling This Assignment:

Create a bullet hole at location of mouse when clicked.
Set an alarm and destroy the hole when it triggers.

145. Rope Between Objects

Difficulty 5/5

Project Outline:

Draw a dangling rope between two instances, allowing the user to move the instances and adjust the length of the rope.

Useful Functions and Built-in Variables:

mouse_x
mouse_y
mouse_check_button_*
draw_circle
draw_line
do
until

Hints on Tackling This Assignment:

Allow player to move two anchors with mouse. Mouse wheel to change rope length. Draw a rope of given length between 2 points.

GAMEMAKER PROGRAMMING CHALLENGES

Difficulty
4/5

146. English to Morse Code

Project Outline:

To convert a string into audio Morse code

Useful Functions and Built-in Variables:

ds_list_create
switch
string_char_at
string_upper
ds_list_size

Hints on Tackling This Assignment:

Convert a string to uppercase and loop through characters using switch adding dots or dashes to a ds_list. Play each dot or dash sound in sequence from the list.

147. Loop Through Instances

Difficulty 3/5

Project Outline:

Use a suitable data structure to create and then destroy a list of instances.

Useful Functions and Built-in Variables:

alarm
ds_list_create
ds_list_add
instance_create_layer
ds_list_size

Hints on Tackling This Assignment:

Populate a ds_list with instances. Display each for two seconds, then destroy and create next. Loop through list again at end.

148. Slowly Rotate To Angle

Difficulty 2/5

Project Outline:

Shoot a missile that rotates and moves towards the mouse cursor's position.

Useful Functions and Built-in Variables:

point_direction
angle_difference
image_angle
direction
mouse_x
mouse_y

Hints on Tackling This Assignment:

Create rotating tower that fires a missile. Make both slowly rotate to the mouse cursor position. Destroy missile when close to cursor position.

149. Draw Clock

Project Outline:

To draw a wall clock with moving hands, that shows the user's current system time.

Useful Functions and Built-in Variables:

current_hour
current_minute
current_second
lengthdir_*
for
draw_line
draw_circle

Hints on Tackling This Assignment:

Draw a clock face with digits. Draw lines for hour, minute and second. Also draw time as formatted text. Use lengthdir_* to calculate end points of lines to draw for each.

150. Randomly Place Objects In Room

Project Outline:

To randomly place a number of instances within the room.

Useful Functions and Built-in Variables:

ds_list_create
ds_list_add
ds_list_size
for
irandom_range
instance_create_layer

Hints on Tackling This Assignment:

Create a list and add instances to it. Use the list to place one of each instance at a random position within the room.

Difficulty
2/5

151. Get Text From Keyboard

Project Outline:

To store a string of characters the user has typed and display this on screen.

Useful Functions and Built-in Variables:

keyboard_check_pressed
keyboard_string
draw_text
vk_enter

Hints on Tackling This Assignment:

Allow user to type and delete text, and display on screen. Allow enter to save text and display on screen, then clear typed text.

152. Shoot Projectile With Gravity

Difficulty 1/5

Project Outline:

To create a moving projectile which is affected by gravity.

Useful Functions and Built-in Variables:

```
image_angle
direction
room_height
gravity
lengthdir_*
```

Hints on Tackling This Assignment:

Spawn a bullet on mouse press at tip of a rotating weapon using lengthdir_* to calculate the spawn point. Set direction, speed and gravity. Update bullet to point direction of travel. Destroy when outside the room.

153. Fade On Player Collision

Difficulty 2/5

Project Outline:

Make an crate that on collision fades and gets destroyed.

Useful Functions and Built-in Variables:

```
place_meeting
instance_destroy
instance_place
with
draw_sprite_ext
```

Hints on Tackling This Assignment:

Move the player with keys. If player collides with a crate, change a flag on create to fade out. When faded out destroy the crate.

GAMEMAKER PROGRAMMING CHALLENGES

Difficulty
3/5

154. Jump On Enemy To Kill

Project Outline:

Create an enemy that is damaged if the player jumps on it from above.

Useful Functions and Built-in Variables:

bbox_top
bbox_bottom
instance_place
vspeed

Hints on Tackling This Assignment:

Check player is above enemy by using bbox_* and vspeed to check it is moving down. If it is destroy the enemy.

Difficulty 3/5

155. Calculate Size Of Area

Project Outline:

To allow the user to click on two locations and create a rectangle. Calculate the area and dimensions of the rectangle and display on screen.

Useful Functions and Built-in Variables:

abs
mouse_x
mouse_y
draw_text
draw_rectangle
mouse_check_button_*

Hints on Tackling This Assignment:

Store position of first and second mouse clicks. Use these values to calculate area, side lengths and perimeter. Also draw as a rectangle.

156. Draw Lines To Mouse Position

Project Outline:

To draw a coloured line from a set position to that of the mouse cursor.

Useful Functions and Built-in Variables:

mouse_x
mouse_y
draw_line_width
draw_set_colour

Hints on Tackling This Assignment:

To draw a coloured line between two points. Use two variables for the start position, and two for the mouse position. Draw lines between these two locations.

157. Random Building Generator

Project Outline:

To make a system that constructs buildings of varying height and colour.

Useful Functions and Built-in Variables:

floor
room_width
irandom_range
for
image_blend
image_index

Hints on Tackling This Assignment:

Use an array to hold random building heights and colours. Use a for loop to place building parts. Use image_blend to set a colour. Add a roof to each building.

158. Queue & Play Audio

Project Outline:

To create list that queues audio and plays the sounds in sequence.

Useful Functions and Built-in Variables:

ds_list_create
ds_list_add
audio_play_sound
audio_is_playing
ds_list_size

Hints on Tackling This Assignment:

Populate a ds_list with audio to play. Play first sound and then delete. When audio stops playing, play next sound if there is one.

159. Boss Style Movement

Difficulty 3/5

Project Outline:

Create a boss enemy with a repeating movement and shooting pattern.

Useful Functions and Built-in Variables:

`path_start`
`alarm`
`instance_create_layer`

Hints on Tackling This Assignment:

Set an enemy to follow a path and shoot 3 bullets. At and of path reset and repeat.

GAMEMAKER PROGRAMMING CHALLENGES

Difficulty
4/5

160. Split Screen

Project Outline:

To make a split screen view, that tracks and follows two players.

Useful Functions and Built-in Variables:

```
keyboard_check
direction speed
instance_place
clamp
```

Hints on Tackling This Assignment:

Create two cars with different keys for movement. Create two views using room view settings and set each to follow a different car.

Difficulty
3/5

161. Check Spelling Of Word

Project Outline:

Allow user to check if a word exists within an included dictionary text file.

Useful Functions and Built-in Variables:

ds_list_create
mouse_check_button
while
file_text_eof
file_text_read_string
ds_list_add

Hints on Tackling This Assignment:

Read each line of a text file into a ds_list by opening a file and using file_text_read_string. Allow user to type in a word. Check if it exists in the list.

Difficulty 3/5

162. Player Character Selection A

Project Outline:

Create a character select screen that scrolls through a selection of sprites.

Useful Functions and Built-in Variables:

`alarm`
`sprite_index`

Hints on Tackling This Assignment:

Display a current sprite character. Use an alarm to change the sprite. Allow mouse button to select and store current option.

163. Weapon Control & Ammo Packs

Difficulty 3/5

Project Outline:

Create a system that keeps tracks of players ammo, which can be reloaded as needed.

Useful Functions and Built-in Variables:

```
global
mouse_check_button_*
draw_sprite
```

Hints on Tackling This Assignment:

Use a global variable to store number of bullets. Reduce by one for each shot. Right click on crate to refill ammo. Draw the appropriate sprite to show ammo.

GAMEMAKER PROGRAMMING CHALLENGES

Difficulty
2/5

164. Follow Player At Distance

Project Outline:

Create a system that moves an enemy to player when further than a set distance from player.

Useful Functions and Built-in Variables:

keyboard_check
distance_to_object
move_towards_point
speed

Hints on Tackling This Assignment:

Allow player to move with WSAD. If enemy is more than a set distance from player, move towards the player with move_towards_point.

165. Resize Based On Position

Difficulty 2/5

Project Outline:

Base a sprites image size on its y position.

Useful Functions and Built-in Variables:

mouse_y
clamp
image_yscale
image_xscale

Hints on Tackling This Assignment:

Change image scale based on y position, so image is small at top of room and larger at bottom. Use mouse_y to calculate and change position.

GAMEMAKER PROGRAMMING CHALLENGES

Difficulty
3/5

166. Using Mouse Wheel To Select Weapon

Project Outline:

To allow player to change the selected weapon by scrolling the mouse wheel up and down.

Useful Functions and Built-in Variables:

mouse_wheel_up
mouse_wheel_down
image_number
draw_sprite

Hints on Tackling This Assignment:

Use mouse wheel to increase and decrease a variable. Keep variable in range of options. Draw image index bases on this variable.

167. Font Drawing From Images

Difficulty 2/5

Project Outline:

To set up and use a font asset created from pre-rendered images.

Useful Functions and Built-in Variables:

font_add_sprite_ext
string_upper
draw_set_font
draw_text

Hints on Tackling This Assignment:

Load in a sprite font with font_add_sprite_ext. Create a string and convert to upper case. Set font and draw the text.

Difficulty 3/5

168. Allow Player To Load Sprite

Project Outline:

Allow the user to select an image from the computer, and to draw this in game.

Useful Functions and Built-in Variables:

get_open_filename
sprite_add
draw_sprite
sprite_delete

Hints on Tackling This Assignment:

Allow player to load a PNG with open_get_filename. Assign to a sprite with sprite_add and draw on screen. Remember to use sprite_delete when no longer needed, to free up memory.

169. Enemy Shoots If Can See Player

Project Outline:

To create a system where the enemy will shoot towards the player is has a direct line of site.

Useful Functions and Built-in Variables:

collision_line
alarm
instance_create_layer
move_towards_point
image_angle sign

Hints on Tackling This Assignment:

Set a flag that changes based on whether it can see the player. Set an alarm to shoot bullet if flag is true. Rotate so the enemy faces the player.

170. Randomly Place Instances

Difficulty 2/5

Project Outline:

To place (n) number of instances within the room, without getting to close to another instances.

Useful Functions and Built-in Variables:

repeat
irandom
instance_nearest
collision_circle
while

Hints on Tackling This Assignment:

Generate random positions that spawn an instance when at least a distance from another using collision circle. Use repeat to place multiple instances and repeat to find an empty position.

171. Split Sentence

Difficulty 4/5

Project Outline:

Use a suitable method to get words from a sentence, and then display them on screen, breaking into lines.

Useful Functions and Built-in Variables:

string_split
for
array_length
string_width

Hints on Tackling This Assignment:

Use string_split to create an array of words. Use a for loop to go through them, Limit the width of each line in pixels, creating line breaks where required.

Difficulty
3/5

172. Simple Menu System

Project Outline:

To create a menu system that takes a player to a different room when a button is clicked with the mouse.

Useful Functions and Built-in Variables:

```
mouse_check_button_*
instance_position
room_goto
```

Hints on Tackling This Assignment:

Create 2-dimensional array to hold button text and target room. Use a variable to loop though options, displaying a button based on value. On press go to target room.

173. Moving Spikes & Damage System

Difficulty
3/5

Project Outline:

To create a spike that fades in and out and gives damage to the player when its alpha is above 0.5.

Useful Functions and Built-in Variables:

audio_is_playing
audio_play_sound
draw_sprite_ext

Hints on Tackling This Assignment:

Use a flag to slowly change an alpha variable for a spike between 0 and 1 and back. If player collides with spike with alpha above 0.5 play a damage sound.

Difficulty
3/5

174. Projectile Spread System

Project Outline:

To create a weapon shooting system that generates a spread of missiles at different angles.

Useful Functions and Built-in Variables:

mouse_x
mouse_y
direction
point_direction
instance_create_layer

Hints on Tackling This Assignment:

Allow mouse button to launch a missile in current weapon direction, plus two more at +20 and -20 degrees, to create a spread effect.

GAMEMAKER PROGRAMMING CHALLENGES

Difficulty
3/5

175. Ball Bounce & Squash

Project Outline:

To give a squashing effect to a ball when it bounces.

Useful Functions and Built-in Variables:

gravity
vspeed
image_yscale

Hints on Tackling This Assignment:

Make a ball that moves with gravity. On collision with a crate squish, then unsquish by changing image_yscale. Make it move back up when unsquished.

Difficulty
3/5

176. Status Effect

Project Outline:

Make the player display what they are doing by drawing text on the screen.

Useful Functions and Built-in Variables:

draw_text

Hints on Tackling This Assignment:

Use a string variable and set this to "idle" if player is not moving, otherwise set string to direction the player is moving.

Difficulty
2/5

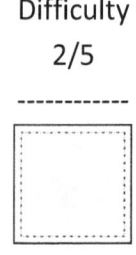

177. Footstep Sounds With Animation

Project Outline:

Create a system that plays footstep audio as the player walks.

Useful Functions and Built-in Variables:

image_index
audio_play_sound
if

Hints on Tackling This Assignment:

Check the current image_index. If it is a certain value, play a footstep sound.

Difficulty
2/5

178. Game Fog

Project Outline:

Overlay the screen with a sprite to create a fog effect that can be turned on and off.

Useful Functions and Built-in Variables:

mouse_check_button_*
draw_sprite_ext

Hints on Tackling This Assignment:

Use a flag that changes between true and false on mouse button pressed. If true overlay the room with a fog image.

179. Destruction With Multiple Subimages

Difficulty 2/5

Project Outline:

Create a destroyable crate with multiple subimages that shows increasing damage and is destroyed when all image frames have been used.

Useful Functions and Built-in Variables:

image_index
image_number
instance_position
mouse_check_button_*

Hints on Tackling This Assignment:

Increase image_index each time instance is clicked with mouse button. On last image destroy the instance.

180. Enemy Hide

Project Outline:

Create a system where enemy seeks cover if the player can see it.

Useful Functions and Built-in Variables:

path_add
mp_grid_create
mp_grid_add_instances
path_start irandom
collision_line

Hints on Tackling This Assignment:

Setup a mp_grid, adding crates as no go area. Set a flag based on if enemy can see player. If it can see, find a random point where it will be hidden. Move on a path to that point.

181. HUD Drawing On GUI Layer

Difficulty
2/5

Project Outline:

Draw a player's info on a GUI layer, so it stays in place as the player moves around room.

Useful Functions and Built-in Variables:

```
lives
score
for
draw_roundrect
draw_sprite
draw_sprite_ext
```

Hints on Tackling This Assignment:

Draw within a Draw GUI Event to draw a room border, lives as images and a bar for hp value.

GAMEMAKER PROGRAMMING CHALLENGES

Difficulty
3/5

182. Scroll Block Of Text Up and Down

Project Outline:

Create a system that draws part of a large text on screen, that can be scrolled up and down.

Useful Functions and Built-in Variables:

```
draw_text
for
string_split
string_width
mouse_wheel_*
array_length
```

Hints on Tackling This Assignment:

Split a string of textinto words, and make sentences of a max length. Use a variable for position, sp that mouse wheel can be used to move text. Draw the text at position.

183. Blood Spray Effect

Difficulty 2/5

Project Outline:

Create an adaptable effect for creating a blood style explosion.

Useful Functions and Built-in Variables:

```
instance_create_layer
repeat
image_angle
direction
```

Hints on Tackling This Assignment:

Spawn multiple blood instances using repeat. Set random, size, direction and speed. Fade over time and destroy when faded.

184. Voice On Level Up

Difficulty 3/5

Project Outline:

Create a system that plays a voice when the level increases or decreases.

Useful Functions and Built-in Variables:

audio_play_sound
clamp

Hints on Tackling This Assignment:

Allow mouse buttons to change a boost variable. Increase / decrease every 10 values, use this to set level. Play level voice when the level changes.

Difficulty
3/5

185. Wind Blown Effect

Project Outline:

Adjust a sprite so that it moves with a wobble as if it is being hit by wind.

Useful Functions and Built-in Variables:

image_angle
sin

Hints on Tackling This Assignment:

Use a sine wave to a make a sprite wobble on it's sprite origin.

GAMEMAKER PROGRAMMING CHALLENGES

Difficulty 3/5

186. Double Jump

Project Outline:

Allow the player jump again whilst in the air.

Useful Functions and Built-in Variables:

gravity
position_meeting
mouse_check_button_*

Hints on Tackling This Assignment:

Create a variable that allows (n) jumps. Use another variable to keep track of jumps. Allow jumping (n) times, then reset count upon collision with floor.

187. Meteor Shower Effect

Difficulty
3/5

Project Outline:

Create a barrage of meteors than explode whilst falling.

Useful Functions and Built-in Variables:

```
repeat
random_range
irandom_range
instance_create_layer
instance_destroy
```

Hints on Tackling This Assignment:

Launch (n) moving meteors with a random count that increments each step. When count reached, destroy and create (n) explosions, that destroy when animation ends.

188. Footstep Dust Effect

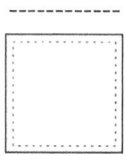

Project Outline:

To create a dust effect when the player character's foot hits the floor.

Useful Functions and Built-in Variables:

floor
image_index
effect_create_layer

Hints on Tackling This Assignment:

Test the current image_index, if it is a certain value, create an effect at position of sprite's foot.

189. Float & Die Effect

Difficulty 3/5

Project Outline:

When an enemy's health has expired, make it turn upside down, float and fade away.

Useful Functions and Built-in Variables:

image_speed
sin
draw_sprite_ext
draw_self
instance_destroy

Hints on Tackling This Assignment:

Use a variable for hp, that reduces. When 0 flip upside-down by changing its y scale to -1, start fading sprite and move up. Use sine wave to give some wobble. Destroy when faded.

190. Fly Level Effect

Project Outline:

To create a plane that can be moved up and down, and returns to middle position when no key is pressed.

Useful Functions and Built-in Variables:

keyboard_check
clamp
room_height

Hints on Tackling This Assignment:

Allow WS to move a plane up and down. When no key is pressed slowly return to middle position.

191. Dash Movement

Difficulty 3/5

Project Outline:

To create a simple dash system that propels the player in the direction it is facing.

Useful Functions and Built-in Variables:

image_xscale
sign
keyboard_check_pressed

Hints on Tackling This Assignment:

Start dash with spacebar pressed. Dash in current direction based on image_xscale, using sign. Count how many steps dashing, and reset when target reached.

192. Sliding On Ice

Difficulty 3/5

Project Outline:

Allow the player to slide when moving on ice, but walk normally on other surfaces.

Useful Functions and Built-in Variables:

keyboard_check
motion_add
hspeed
clamp

Hints on Tackling This Assignment:

Allow AD to move. Set a flag to true when on ice, false otherwise. If on ice reduce speed slowly by slowly reducing hspeed. If not on ice set speed to 0 when not moving.

Difficulty
1/5

193. Underwater Effect

Project Outline:

To use a combination of layer effects and sprites to create an underwater scene.

Useful Functions and Built-in Variables:	**Hints on Tackling This Assignment:**
No code	Create a room with a background of water, place some sprites on an asset layer. Use GameMaker's built in effect layer to create an underwater effects.

194. Hint Arrow To Direction Of Powerup

Project Outline:

To use a sprite indicator that points in the direction of the nearest power-up.

Useful Functions and Built-in Variables:

instance_exists
instance_nearest
point_direction
angle_difference
sign

Hints on Tackling This Assignment:

If a power-up exists, get the nearest, and it's angle from the player. Slowly rotate a sprite around the player, based on players position, to point towards the power-up.

Difficulty
2/5

195. Button To Open Website

Project Outline:

To allow the user to click a button that opens up a webpage.

Useful Functions and Built-in Variables:

url_open
mouse_check_button_*

Hints on Tackling This Assignment:

Create a simple button, that when clicked opens up a webpage.

196. Health Pack Slowly Increase Health

Project Outline:

Make a system that slowly increases health to a target value when a health pack is collected.

Useful Functions and Built-in Variables:

health
mouse_check_button_*
instance_position
instance_destroy

Hints on Tackling This Assignment:

Set health and target amount to start. When player clicks on health pack, increase target and destroy pack. Slowly increase health to match target.

197. Change Enemy Colour When Targeted

Difficulty 3/5

Project Outline:

To create a system that visually shows when a player has targeted an enemy, by giving the sprite a red tinge.

Useful Functions and Built-in Variables:

alarm
mouse_check_button_*
draw_sprite_ext
draw_self

Hints on Tackling This Assignment:

On mouse click randomly select an enemy. Show this by drawing enemy with a red colour using draw_sprite_ext.

Difficulty
3/5

198. Limit Weapon Shooting Timer

Project Outline:

Make a player's weapon have a cool-down timer that limits how often it can used.

Useful Functions and Built-in Variables:

alarm

Hints on Tackling This Assignment:

Use a flag and alarm to determine when player can shoot. Shoot if flag is true, then set false and set an alarm. Upon alarm triggering, set flag back to true.

199. Clock Stopwatch

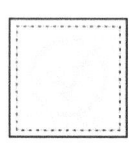

Difficulty 4/5

Project Outline:

To create a stopwatch that can be started, stopped and restarted, and reset. Give an accuracy of 100ths of a second.

Useful Functions and Built-in Variables:

game_set_speed
mouse_check_button_*
string_repeat
floor
mod

Hints on Tackling This Assignment:

Set game speed to make calculations easier. Left mouse to start/pause/restart. Right button to reset. Increase timer when running and format text and draw.

200. Weapon Power & Direction System

Difficulty 3/5

Project Outline:

Allow a user to interact with a single mouse button, to select the direction and speed of a projectile.

Useful Functions and Built-in Variables:

```
enum
mouse_check_button
instance_create_layer
```

Hints on Tackling This Assignment:

Create a basic state machine with an enum. Start with weapon rotating. Upon mouse click change to strength. Upon next click shoot bullet with angle and strength.

Difficulty
5/5

201. Moving A Platform Left and Right

Project Outline:

Create a movement system that moves the player when standing on a moving platform.

Useful Functions and Built-in Variables:

instance_position
gravity
vspeed

Hints on Tackling This Assignment:

Make a basic movement and jumping system. If player is standing on a moving platform, update player's x position. Do this by checking for collision with a platform, if true move player in same direction platform is moving.

202. Spin Around Other Instance

Project Outline:

To make a sprite orbit another.

Useful Functions and Built-in Variables:

lengthdir_*
draw_sprite_ext

Hints on Tackling This Assignment:

Move the player with mouse, calculate position of orbiting sprite using lengthdir_*, gradually changing the angle, and draw it.

203. Vehicle With Smooth Turning

Difficulty 4/5

Project Outline:

To create a smooth turning system, with wheels that rotate to planned direction.

Useful Functions and Built-in Variables:

lengthdir_*
image_angle
draw_sprite_ext
angle_difference

Hints on Tackling This Assignment:

Keep track of current angle, and set a target based on input. Use lengthdir_* to set position to draw the wheels.

204. Tank and Turret Movement

Difficulty 3/5

Project Outline:

To create a tank and turret system, where each element can be rotated independently. Ensure turret remains attached to the tank.

Useful Functions and Built-in Variables:

```
instance_create_layer
mouse_check_button
lengthdir_*
image_angle
draw_sprite_ext
```

Hints on Tackling This Assignment:

Create turret from the tank and send through id so turret knows which instance to stay attached to. Use lengthdir_* to calculate position to spawn bullet.

205. Bbox Collision

Difficulty 2/5

Project Outline:

To draw bounding boxes of several instances, and to draw the instance id upon collision.

Useful Functions and Built-in Variables:

bbox_*
draw_rectangle
instance_place

Hints on Tackling This Assignment:

Move the player and use instance_place to detect a collision. Use draw_rectangle to draw the bounding box.

206. NPC That Performs Tasks

Difficulty 4/5

Project Outline:

Create a farming NPC that plants seeds, waters them and picks fruit. Also takes a break when they get tired.

Useful Functions and Built-in Variables:

enum
speed
alarm
move_towards_point
instance_position
position_meeting

Hints on Tackling This Assignment:

Use an enum based state machine. Randomly set a task to perform. Create soil that needs seeds, watering and picking. Gradually reduce NPC HP, requiring visit to a Café to replenish HP.

207. Wall Jumping

Difficulty 3/5

Project Outline:

To create a system that allows a player to jump off vertical walls.

Useful Functions and Built-in Variables:

gravity
vspeed
place_meeting
keyboard_check

Hints on Tackling This Assignment:

Detect when player is next to a wall, if it is allow jumping by increasing vspeed.

GAMEMAKER PROGRAMMING CHALLENGES

Difficulty
3/5

208. Weapon Upgrade System

Project Outline:

To create a system that provides the player with a temporary weapon upgrade.

Useful Functions and Built-in Variables:

```
alarm
instance_create_layer
speed
direction
```

Hints on Tackling This Assignment:

Use a flag for weapon upgrade. On input, set to true and start an alarm, which resets flag on trigger. When true, draw additional weapons that shoot multiple projectiles.

209. Player Shield System

Difficulty 3/5

Project Outline:

To allow the player to equip a shield system that prevents damage.

Useful Functions and Built-in Variables:

```
mask_index
draw_sprite_ext
effect_create_layer
```

Hints on Tackling This Assignment:

Allow mouse button to activiate player's shield. When enemy missile hits player, prevent damage when shield is active.

GAMEMAKER PROGRAMMING CHALLENGES

Difficulty
3/5

210. Sprite Stacking Fake 3D

Project Outline:

To create a fake 3D effect by stacking sprites on top of each other.

Useful Functions and Built-in Variables:

point_direction
for
lengthdir_*
draw_sprite_ext

Hints on Tackling This Assignment:

To draw sprites of decreasing sizes on top of each other for a 3D effect. Use a for loop and point_direction to set position and sizes of sprites to draw.

211. Water Reflection Using Effect Layers

Difficulty 4/5

Project Outline:

To use one of GameMaker's built-in water effect layer to create a water reflection.

Useful Functions and Built-in Variables:

sprite_index
instance_create_layer
image_yscale

Hints on Tackling This Assignment:

Create an instance above an effect layer. When created, create another instance below the effect layer, with yscale set as -1. Use a water effect layer on this instance to create an underwater effect.

212. Magnet System

Difficulty 3/5

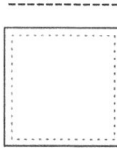

Project Outline:

To create a magnet that attracts nearby instances.

Useful Functions and Built-in Variables:

point_direction
point_distance
with
motion_add
draw_circle

Hints on Tackling This Assignment:

Create a magnet with a range drawn as a circle. If player gets within range, add motion on the player to move towards magnet.

GAMEMAKER PROGRAMMING CHALLENGES

Difficulty
3/5

213. Health Heart Part System

Project Outline:

Draw player's health using quarter sprites of a heart.

Useful Functions and Built-in Variables:

health
clamp
div
for
mod
draw_sprite
mouse_check_button_*

Hints on Tackling This Assignment:

Set a starting health and max health variable. Use div and mod to calculate how many whole health sprites and parts. Use a loop to draw whole, then parts.

214. Tap To Move System

Difficulty 3/5

Project Outline:

To create a system that moves the player, based on how fast they can tap a button.

Useful Functions and Built-in Variables:

mouse_check_button_*
image_speed

Hints on Tackling This Assignment:

Create a variable for tracking taps. Increase on mouse button pressed. Reduce variable each step. Use variable to animate.

215. Resize Sprite

Difficulty 3/5

Project Outline:

To allow the user to click and move the mouse so it resizes the sprite.

Useful Functions and Built-in Variables:

mouse_check_button_*
mouse_x
mouse_y
draw_sprite_ext

Hints on Tackling This Assignment:

Allow user to click one position and store it, then a second position. Use positions to draw a sprite.

Difficulty 5/5

216. Moving Platform Up and Down

Project Outline:

To allow a player to move up and down when positioned on a moving platform.

Useful Functions and Built-in Variables:

position_meeting
vspeed

Hints on Tackling This Assignment:

Use a variable that switches between 1 and -1 after a distance to move floor up and down. to detect collision with floor. Have a player that moves up and down as the floor moves.

217. Rotating Wheel

Difficulty 4/5

Project Outline:

To create a "wheel of fortune" that spins and slows down, landing on a segment at random.

Useful Functions and Built-in Variables:

draw_sprite
draw_text
image_angle
audio_play_sound
audio_sound_pitch
lengthdir_*

Hints on Tackling This Assignment:

Spin a wheel that rotates and slows down by changing angle. Adjust a playing sound pitch based on wheel speed. Use wheel angle to determine final position.

218. Fake 3D

Project Outline:

To create a 3D effect by scaling images based on their y position.

Useful Functions and Built-in Variables:

image_speed
image_index
vspeed
image_angle
clamp
abs
sign
draw_sprite_ext

Hints on Tackling This Assignment:

Spawn trees above room top, increase vspeed and size as they fall. Use clamp to keep in range. Draw a car at bottom that rotates a bit when moving.

Difficulty
4/5

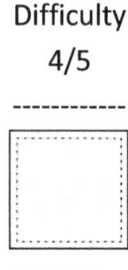

219. Flame Effect Using Particles

Project Outline:

To use a particle system to create a flame effect.

Useful Functions and Built-in Variables:

part_system_create
part_type_*
part_particles_create
part_system_drawit

Hints on Tackling This Assignment:

An example showing a basic effect using particles. Create a stream of particles that moves up so it looks like a flame.

Difficulty 3/5

220. Rotating Spaceship With Inertia

Project Outline:

To create a moveable spaceship that has inertia.

Useful Functions and Built-in Variables:

```
friction
clamp
motion_add
keyboard_check
move_wrap
image_angle
```

Hints on Tackling This Assignment:

Set up a ship with friction. Allow keys for rotating ship angle. Another key for motion_add to apply impulse in direction. move_wrap to wrap on room.

Difficulty
4/5

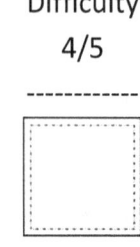

221. Weapon and Manually Select Target

Project Outline:

To create a space ship that can be moved, with a weapon that locks on to an enemy that the player clicks on.

Useful Functions and Built-in Variables:

instance_create_layer
point_direction
angle_difference
lengthdir_*
sign
id

Hints on Tackling This Assignment:

Create a ship with WSAD controls. Attach a weapon to ship which can target an enemy when enemy is clicked. Allow clicking again to deselect. Rotate weapon to face enemy. Draw a green border around selected enemy.

222. Destructible Terrain

Difficulty 4/5

Project Outline:

Use a sprite created from a surface that allows the player to make holes in it by dropping a bomb.

Useful Functions and Built-in Variables:

surface_create
surface_set_target
surface_reset_target
surface_free
sprite_create_from_surface
sprite_delete

Hints on Tackling This Assignment:

Assign a terrain sprite to an object instance. When colliding with a bomb, create a surface and remove a section to show damage. Create a sprite from the surface and assign to the instance.

Difficulty
3/5

223. Horizontal Scrolling Menu

Project Outline:

To create smoothly scrolling horizontal menu that the player can select an option using the mouse wheel.

Useful Functions and Built-in Variables:

array_length
mouse_wheel_*
instance_create_layer
floor

Hints on Tackling This Assignment:

Use an array to save button text. Use mouse to change button target. Display buttons, and slowly move horizontally to target option.

Difficulty
3/5

224. Vertical Scrolling Menu

Project Outline:

To create smoothly scrolling vertical menu that the player can select an option using the mouse wheel.

Useful Functions and Built-in Variables:

array_length
mouse_wheel_*
instance_create_layer
floor

Hints on Tackling This Assignment:

Use an array to save button text. Use mouse to change button target. Display buttons, and slowly move vertically to target option.

225. Ladder Climbing

Difficulty 4/5

Project Outline:

To create a system for a platformer game that allows the player to climb up and down a ladder.

Useful Functions and Built-in Variables:

place_meeting
gravity
vspeed
keyboard_check

Hints on Tackling This Assignment:

Use a flag to determine player is colliding with a ladder. Allow WS to move up and down ladder. Add a system that allows jumping and falling when over a ladder.

226. Attack Left and Right

Difficulty 2/5

Project Outline:

Create an attacking system that attacks in the direction the player is facing, then in the opposite direction.

Useful Functions and Built-in Variables:

sprite_index
image_xscale
image_index

Hints on Tackling This Assignment:

Allow AD to change directions. On mouse click run animation by changing sprite_index. At animation end event, change xscale, repeat and then reset.

Difficulty
4/5

227. Moving Grass Side View

Project Outline:

To create some grass that moves upon collision with the player.

Useful Functions and Built-in Variables:

place_meeting
image_angle
sprite_index
choose

Hints on Tackling This Assignment:

Spawn some grass blades across bottom of room using a for loop. Upon collision with player, slowly move grass in random direction. Return to angle when no contact.

228. Target Enemy With Highest HP

Project Outline:

To create a weapon that seeks out the enemy with the highest hp.

Useful Functions and Built-in Variables:

alarm
ds_priority_create
ds_priority_add
ds_priority_delete
with

Hints on Tackling This Assignment:

Use with to add instances to a priority list. Sort by highest hp and choose this as a target. Use an alarm to repeat this, again targeting an enemy with max hp.

Difficulty
4/5

229. Rotating Mini Map

Project Outline:

To draw a mini map with nearby instances, that rotates based on players direction of movement.

Useful Functions and Built-in Variables:

```
with
point_distance
point_direction
draw_sprite_ext
lengthdir_*
```

Hints on Tackling This Assignment:

Allow player to choose to rotate map or not. Use with to get wall instances. Get direction and distance from player. Use lengthdir_* to place blips.

230. Screen Flash Damage Indicator

Project Outline:

Splash a colour over the screen when the player takes damage.

Useful Functions and Built-in Variables:

instance_destroy
draw_set_alpha
draw_set_colour
draw_rectangle
choose

Hints on Tackling This Assignment:

On mouse button pressed change a flag to true, create flash instances when true. Draw a rectangle over room in random colour and fade out.

231. Board Game Move Pieces A

Difficulty 4/5

Project Outline:

To create a system where a die is rolled and moves a player piece around the board.

Useful Functions and Built-in Variables:

move_towards_point
point_distance
enum

Hints on Tackling This Assignment:

Create a state machine with enum. To wait, move and end turn. Upon button press, roll a die and move that number of squares.

232. Board Game Move Pieces B

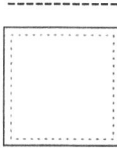

Project Outline:

To roll a dice and move to a new position.

Useful Functions and Built-in Variables:

move_towards_point
point_distance

Hints on Tackling This Assignment:

An example without an enum. Upon button press, roll a die and move the total number of squares in one go.

233. Predict Path Of Projectile

Project Outline:

To calculate path of a trajectory and draw it visually.

Useful Functions and Built-in Variables:

ds_list_create
mouse_check_button
ds_list_delete
for
draw_circle

Hints on Tackling This Assignment:

Uses a script the Motin Prediect Script from GMLscripts.com: https://gmlscripts.com/script/motion_predict to get a set of points for a moving instance. Use a for loop to iterate through the points and draw with draw_circle.

234. Animated Mouth When Talking

Project Outline:

To create a mouth that changes size and shape when a condition is true.

Useful Functions and Built-in Variables:

random_range
mouse_check_button
draw_sprite_ext

Hints on Tackling This Assignment:

When mouse button down, slowly randomize image x and y scale. When released, slowly reset.

235. Move All Instances By Given Amount

Difficulty 2/5

Project Outline:

To allow movement of all instances by a given amount.

Useful Functions and Built-in Variables:

```
with
all
keyboard_check_pressed
```

Hints on Tackling This Assignment:

When a WSAD if pressed, use with all to move all instances in room by a given amount.

236. Split Rocks and Rotate

Project Outline:

To allow player to click on a rotating asteroid, breaking it into smaller pieces.

Useful Functions and Built-in Variables:

instance_create_layer
instance_destroy
move_wrap
mouse_check_button_*

Hints on Tackling This Assignment:

Set a large rock to move in random directions and spin. On mouse button pressed, split into two smaller rocks.

Difficulty
4/5

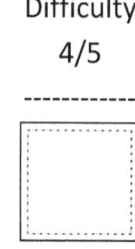

237. Multiple Missiles – Only Target If Not

Project Outline:

To create a missile system where the missiles only target an instance if another missile is not already targeting it.

Useful Functions and Built-in Variables:

noone
with
move_towards_point
point_direction
angle_difference

Hints on Tackling This Assignment:

Create a missile, and use with to look for an enemy not already targeted, using a flag. If targeted change colour. Missile to look for targets each step.

GAMEMAKER PROGRAMMING CHALLENGES

Difficulty
3/5

238. Find a Path Through A Maze

Project Outline:

To plot a path through a maze, whilst avoiding instances.

Useful Functions and Built-in Variables:

mp_grid_create
mp_grid_add_instances
path_add path_start
mp_grid_path

Hints on Tackling This Assignment:

Create a grid with mp_grid_create and add instances for no-go areas. Plot a path with mp_grid_path, then start an instance on that path.

239. Flying Instance With Shadow

Difficulty 2/5

Project Outline:

To draw a moving instance with a drop shadow.

Useful Functions and Built-in Variables:

path_start
draw_self
draw_sprite_ext

Hints on Tackling This Assignment:

Start a instance on a path to move around the room. Use draw_sprite to draw the instance, and draw a shadow at x and y offset and a black colour.

Difficulty 2/5

240. Cover Whole Room With Instances

Project Outline:

To calculate where to place instances so the whole room is covered.

Useful Functions and Built-in Variables:

```
for
instance_create_layer
sprite_get_width
sprite_get_height
room_width
room_height
```

Hints on Tackling This Assignment:

Get the sprite and room dimensions and calculate how many sprites are needed in each direction. Use a nested for loop to place instances in the room.

241. Keyboard Controlled Player With Mouse Controlled Gun

Difficulty 3/5

Project Outline:

To allow the player to move with the keyboard, and target a gun using the mouse.

Useful Functions and Built-in Variables:

draw_self
draw_sprite_ext
keyboard_check
point_direction

Hints on Tackling This Assignment:

Move the player with AD. Point the gun using angle from player to mouse position. Draw player then draw gun, adjusting xscale to keep the gun sprite correct regardless of side.

Difficulty
3/5

242. Spaceship Control

Project Outline:

A space ship with inertia movement with gravity.

Useful Functions and Built-in Variables:

keyboard_check
motion_add
room_width
hspeed
vspeed

Hints on Tackling This Assignment:

Use keys WAD to add motion with motion_add.
Add gravity by adding downwards motion each step.
Keep within room boundaries.

243. Slide In Buttons

Difficulty 3/5

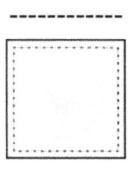

Project Outline:

To slide in some buttons without using a sequence.

Useful Functions and Built-in Variables:

```
point_distance
move_towards_point
speed
```

Hints on Tackling This Assignment:

Start a button outside room and move towards a preset position. When reached, stop moving.

Difficulty 3/5

244. Draw Crosshair In Middle Of View

Project Outline:

To draw a crosshair that stays centered, even when the view moves.

Useful Functions and Built-in Variables:

camera_get_view_x
camera_get_view_y
camera_get_view_width
camera_get_view_height
draw_line draw_circle

Hints on Tackling This Assignment:

Calculate the center of the current view and draw a crosshair with circle and lines.

245. Draw Rectangle With Dashed Border

Difficulty 2/5

Project Outline:

Create a script that draws a rectangle of a given size with a dashed border.

Useful Functions and Built-in Variables:

irandom_range

Hints on Tackling This Assignment:

Uses script: https://gmlscripts.com/script/draw_rectangle_dashed Create a rectangle at a random position and size. Send coordinates to the script.

246. Top Down 360 Degree Movement

Project Outline:

To create a 360 degree movement system that prevents walking through instances.

Useful Functions and Built-in Variables:

keyboard_check
speed
instance_place
point_direction
lengthdir_*

Hints on Tackling This Assignment:

Allow AD to rotate player, and WS to move forward / backward in current direction. Use lengthdir_* to check for collision, if there is, move away.

247. Attacking Sprite Control System

Difficulty 3/5

Project Outline:

To allow a player to attack in the direction it is facing, and return to an idle animation after attack is completed.

Useful Functions and Built-in Variables:

sprite_index
image_index
image_xscale

Hints on Tackling This Assignment:

AD to change direction. Left mouse button to attack. Use a flag for attacking. Set when attack starts and reset on animation end.

Difficulty 4/5

248. Enemy Patrol System

Project Outline:

Create an enemy that patrols along a path, which turns to face the player if in line of sight.

Useful Functions and Built-in Variables:

path_start
lengthdir_*
image_angle
point_in_triangle
draw_triangle

Hints on Tackling This Assignment:

Start player on path. Use point_in_triangle to check if player is within a zone, if it is point in direction of player.

249. Change Cursor To Selected Item

Difficulty 3/5

Project Outline:

Create a system where a player can select an item, draw this instead of mouse_cursor, and allow placement of an instance in the room with this sprite.

Useful Functions and Built-in Variables:

mouse_check_button_pressed
keyboard_check_pressed
window_set_cursor
draw_sprite

Hints on Tackling This Assignment:

Set keys 0 to 3 and choose sprite. On mouse click place an instance in the room with this sprite assigned to it.

250. Fade Between Text Messages

Difficulty 3/5

Project Outline:

To gradually fade in and out between two messages.

Useful Functions and Built-in Variables:

draw_set_font
draw_set_alpha

Hints on Tackling This Assignment:

Set a value to gradually change a value between 0 and 1. Use this to set the alpha of a text and another text with 1 minus this value to fade between two texts.

Difficulty 3/5

251. Enemy Jumping

Project Outline:

To make an enemy jump when it collides with a certain instance.

Useful Functions and Built-in Variables:

gravity
vspeed
sprite_index
instance_position

Hints on Tackling This Assignment:

Create some basic movement and jumping code. Set instance moving and change direction on room border. When colliding with a block, make it jump by setting a negative vspeed.

252. Pick Up and Place Items

Difficulty 4/5

Project Outline:

To allow the player to pick-up up to three items and then drop them. Store picked up items in an inventory.

Useful Functions and Built-in Variables:

array_push
array_length
instance_create_layer

Hints on Tackling This Assignment:

Create an array for all items, and for picked up items. Allow key presses to pick up and drop items. Limit holding to three items, dropping one if more than this.

253. 360 Degree Laser

Difficulty 3/5

Project Outline:

To create a system that draws a laser using a sprite, from a weapon to the mouse position.

Useful Functions and Built-in Variables:

point_distance
point_direction
mouse_x
mouse_y
lengthdir_*
draw_sprite_general

Hints on Tackling This Assignment:

Get distance and angle from weapon to mouse position. Calculate how many laser sprite parts are needed. Draw them and then a Use a different sprite for the final position.

254. Laser Through Multiple Instances

Project Outline:

To create a laser that can pass through multiple instances and make them glow red if hit.

Useful Functions and Built-in Variables:

draw_sprite_ext
ds_list_size for
ds_list_create
ds_list_clear
collision_line_list

Hints on Tackling This Assignment:

Use collision_line_list to get all ids of enemy instances colliding with enemy. If enemy is in the list, draw with a red colour.

255. Draw Sprite On Sprite Layer

Difficulty 1/5

Project Outline:

To allow mouse button to place and remove a sprite on an asset layer.

Useful Functions and Built-in Variables:

layer_sprite_create
layer_sprite_destroy
mouse_check_button_*

Hints on Tackling This Assignment:

Allow left mouse button to place a sprite on an asset layer, right button to remove it.

Difficulty
3/5

256. Detect Single Or Double Mouse Button Click

Project Outline:

Detect a single or double based on quickly a mouse button is pressed.

Useful Functions and Built-in Variables:

mouse_check_button_*
if

Hints on Tackling This Assignment:

Start a timer when mouse button clicked. If timer reaches over half a second, record as single click. If pressed again in under half a second, record as double click. Show text of the outcome.

257. Leave Path To Attack Then Return To Path

Difficulty 4/5

Project Outline:

To create a system where an enemy follows a path. Allow the enemy to move away from the path to attack, then return to the path and continue on it.

Useful Functions and Built-in Variables:

path_start
mouse_x mouse_y
path_position
path_end
move_towards_point
point_distance

Hints on Tackling This Assignment:

Start an instance on a path. When mouse is clicked, get the position. Stop path and move to point, then return to position, and continue path at same place.

Difficulty
4/5

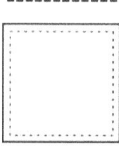

258. Choose Random Word

Project Outline:

To store all words from a dictionary text file and choose one word of a given length at random.

Useful Functions and Built-in Variables:

ds_list_create
while
file_text_eof
file_text_read_string
ds_list_add
ds_list_size
file_text_readln
do until
string_length

Hints on Tackling This Assignment:

Load words from a dictionary text into an array. On keypress choose random words until word of required length is found, and display on screen.

259. Change Sprite When Jumping

Difficulty 2/5

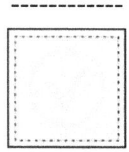

Project Outline:

To change a player's sprite when jumping or falling.

Useful Functions and Built-in Variables:

sprite_index
vspeed
position_meeting

Hints on Tackling This Assignment:

Set sprite as idle when on the ground. Set a different sprite when jumping and falling.

GAMEMAKER PROGRAMMING CHALLENGES

Difficulty
1/5

260. Play Random Sound

Project Outline:

To choose and play a random sound from a selection.

Useful Functions and Built-in Variables:

keyboard_check_pressed
choose
audio_play_sound
mouse_check_button

Hints on Tackling This Assignment:

Upon a key press use choose to select a random sound. Then play the sound with audio_play_sound.

261. Move Multiple Instances Through A Small Gap

Difficulty 4/5

Project Outline:

To create a system that allows multiple instances to move through a small gap, without overlapping

Useful Functions and Built-in Variables:

other
point_direction
lengthdir_*

Hints on Tackling This Assignment:

When an enemy collides with another enemy or wall, get the distance and direction between them and move a little in opposite direction.

262. Draw Text With Formatting

Difficulty 2/5

Project Outline:

To create a function that can be called to draw formatted text with a single line.

Useful Functions and Built-in Variables:

draw_set_font
draw_set_colour
draw_set_halign
draw_set_valign
draw_text

Hints on Tackling This Assignment:

Create a function that takes in text and formatting variables. Use this script to draw text on screen.

263. Moving Grass Top Down

Project Outline:

To create an effect that moves grass when an instance moves through it.

Useful Functions and Built-in Variables:

choose
sprite_index
image_angle
floor
image_xscale

Hints on Tackling This Assignment:

Make a blade of grass with a random subimage, and slowly move in a random direction upon collision with the player. Slowly move back when collision ends.

264. Turn Before Moving

Project Outline:

Create a system that moves an instance on a path, pausing when changing direction.

Useful Functions and Built-in Variables:

path_start
angle_difference
abs
direction
sign
image_angle
path_speed

Hints on Tackling This Assignment:

Start moving on path. If there is a difference between current image_angle and direction, pause path and rotate angle. When below a value, resume path.

265. Alert Player To Low Health

Difficulty 3/5

Project Outline:

To create an audio and visual system that alerts the player when their health is low.

Useful Functions and Built-in Variables:

```
alarm
health
audio_play_sound
image_xscale
image_yscale
```

Hints on Tackling This Assignment:

Check the current health, if below a threshold set a flag to true. When true change image scale up and down to make it pulse.

266. Avatar Creator A

Difficulty 4/5

Project Outline:

Create a system that allows the user to create an avatar using a selection of face parts. Save as a sprite that can be used in-game

Useful Functions and Built-in Variables:

sprite_get_number
string
string_repeat
draw_text draw_sprite
sprite_create_from_surface
surface_create
surface_free
sprite_delete

Hints on Tackling This Assignment:

Create a button for each face feature that changes subimage on click. Add a button that creates a surface and draws all parts, then saves as a sprite.

GAMEMAKER PROGRAMMING CHALLENGES

Difficulty
3/5

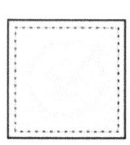

267. Ship Shooting Cannon Balls

Project Outline:

To create a rotating ship that fires cannon balls from the correct positions.

Useful Functions and Built-in Variables:

draw_circle
lengthdir_*
instance_create_layer

Hints on Tackling This Assignment:

Create a basic rotating ship. Fire projectiles by using lengthdir_* to find ship center points, then again for firing position. Shoot cannon balls at 90' from ship angle.

GAMEMAKER PROGRAMMING CHALLENGES

Difficulty
3/5

268. Simple Glow Effect With Circles

Project Outline:

To create a light glow effect using circles.

Useful Functions and Built-in Variables:

draw_set_colour
draw_set_alpha
draw_circle

Hints on Tackling This Assignment:

Slowly change a size variable between min and max ranges. Use this value to draw circles with alpha for a changing glow effect.

GAMEMAKER PROGRAMMING CHALLENGES

Difficulty
3/5

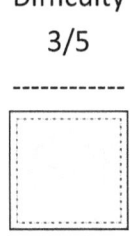

269. Simple Glow Effect With Sprite A

Project Outline:

To create a glow effect by changing a sprites size.

Useful Functions and Built-in Variables:

draw_sprite_ext

Hints on Tackling This Assignment:

Change the image scsale of a sprite between min and max sizes to create a pulsing glow effect.

Difficulty
3/5

270. Simple Glow Effect With Sprite B

Project Outline:

Use two different sprites to create a glow effect.

Useful Functions and Built-in Variables:

draw_sprite_ext

Hints on Tackling This Assignment:

Create a variable that slowly changes between min and max ranges. Use this value to scale two sprites of different sizes to create a glowing effect.

271. Move To Target Then Stop

Difficulty 2/5

Project Outline:

To move an instance to a target position, slowing down as it gets closer to target, then stops.

Useful Functions and Built-in Variables:

mouse_x
mouse_y
point_distance
move_towards_point
speed

Hints on Tackling This Assignment:

On mouse click set a target position and flag. Whilst flag is true, move towards this point until close, and then snap in place and reset flag.

GAMEMAKER PROGRAMMING CHALLENGES

Difficulty
2/5

272. Level Based On Score

Project Outline:

To develop an upgrade system that increases the level for every 1000 points.

Useful Functions and Built-in Variables:

clamp
div
draw_text

Hints on Tackling This Assignment:

Use div on the score value to determine level. Draw score and level on screen.

273. Player Control Information

Difficulty 3/5

Project Outline:

To develop a system that shows player controls for the first five times the game is played.

Useful Functions and Built-in Variables:

ini_open
file_exists
ini_read_real
ini_close
ini_write_real
file_delete

Hints on Tackling This Assignment:

Load and save a value to an ini file. Increase the value each game. When below 5 display a message, when above do not draw. Reset with right button.

GAMEMAKER PROGRAMMING CHALLENGES

Difficulty
2/5

274. Selectable Backgrounds

Project Outline:

To let the player choose from a selection of backgrounds.

Useful Functions and Built-in Variables:

keyboard_check_pressed
layer_get_id
layer_background_get_id
layer_background_sprite

Hints on Tackling This Assignment:

On keyboard presses of keys 1 2 3 4, set a different background. Get background id with layer_get_id and layer_background_get_id. Set with layer_background_sprite.

275. Draw Buttons With Chosen Language

Difficulty 3/5

Project Outline:

To use a suitable data structure to store words in different languages, and allow the player to choose a language.

Useful Functions and Built-in Variables:

keyboard_check_pressed
mouse_check_button
draw_text

Hints on Tackling This Assignment:

Set up a 2D array with different languages for use in buttons. Allow keypress of A to change a variable for language. Draw buttons with selected language displayed.

276. Lottery Numbers Selector

Difficulty 3/5

Project Outline:

To randomly choose a selection of lottery balls, and to draw them on screen with appropriate coloured background.

Useful Functions and Built-in Variables:

ds_list_create
for
draw_set_colour
draw_circle
ds_list_add draw_text
ds_list_shuffle

Hints on Tackling This Assignment:

Create a list and use a for loop to populate with numbers 1 to 50. Shuffle the list and take the first 6 items and place in a new list. Draw a coloured circle based on value, and draw text.

Difficulty
3/5

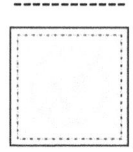

277. Draw View Border On Draw Event

Project Outline:

To draw a border based on the current view, updating if the view changes position.

Useful Functions and Built-in Variables:

camera_get_view_*
draw_roundrect

Hints on Tackling This Assignment:

Use camera_get_* functions to get current view size and position. Use a border size variable, and draw a round rectangle on screen. Use normal draw event, not GUI.

278. Card Flipping Animation

Project Outline:

To create a graphical effect that shows a card flipping from back to front.

Useful Functions and Built-in Variables:

sprite_index
image_xscale

Hints on Tackling This Assignment:

Use variable definitions for the example's card face. Start showing back and reduce x scale until 0, then change sprite and increase scale back to 1.

279. Day Night Cycle

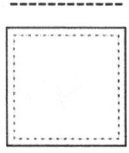

Difficulty
3/5

Project Outline:

To tint the room based on the time of day.

Useful Functions and Built-in Variables:

alarm
switch case
draw_set_alpha
draw_set_colour
draw_rectangle

Hints on Tackling This Assignment:

Create a value for hours that increases with an alarm. Use a switch case system to set alpha and colour based on time. Draw a rectangle overview with settings.

GAMEMAKER PROGRAMMING CHALLENGES

Difficulty
4/5

280. Draw Rotating Shapes

Project Outline:

To draw a square, star and triangle that rotate, using draw_line.

Useful Functions and Built-in Variables:

lengthdir_*
draw_line

Hints on Tackling This Assignment:

Set up a variable for rotation that increases each step.
Use lengthdir_* functions to rotate a set of points.
Draw lines between points to make rotating shapes.

281. Positional Audio

Difficulty 3/5

Project Outline:

To play audio from left or right speaker, depending on direction and distance.

Useful Functions and Built-in Variables:

audio_play_sound_at
audio_listener_position
audio_listener_orientation

Hints on Tackling This Assignment:

Set an object in room and use audio_play_sound_at to start playing a looping sound. Set audio_listener_* as the player moves, to change audio levels.

Difficulty
3/5

282. Imploding Text Effect

Project Outline:

To take letters from a string and implode them from room border into position to make a sentence.

Useful Functions and Built-in Variables:

```
string_length
string_char_at
point_distance
move_towards_point
for
```

Hints on Tackling This Assignment:

Get length of a string and loop through each character with a for loop and string_char_at. Send to a new instance that moves to a target position to show the string.

283. Laser Collision Effect

Difficulty 3/5

Project Outline:

To make a laser that fires when an instance is present along its direction. Also show damage effect when instance is hit.

Useful Functions and Built-in Variables:

point_direction
distance_to_point
for
lengthdir_*
effect_create_layer
draw_line

Hints on Tackling This Assignment:

Get distance and direction to mouse. Use a for loop and collision_line to look for a collision. If found, save distance and draw effect and laser line.

284. Pop Up Message

Project Outline:

To display a random message when an instance is interacted with.

Useful Functions and Built-in Variables:

position_meeting
mouse_x
mouse_y
irandom
array_length
draw_text

Hints on Tackling This Assignment:

Add some short messages to an array. Use a flag that sets when mouse over instance or not. When set to true, choose a random message and display it.

Difficulty
3/5

285. Skill Points

Project Outline:

Allow a player to spend points to increase stats. Limit number of points each attribute can have.

Useful Functions and Built-in Variables:

`instance_create_layer`
`for`
`mouse_check_button_*`
`draw_text`

Hints on Tackling This Assignment:

Populate a 2D array with names and stats points (i.e. Magic, Wisdom). Create buttons that add values to these stats.

Difficulty 3/5

286. Depth Based Movement

Project Outline:

To make a depth system that allows a player to move in front of and behind other instances.

Useful Functions and Built-in Variables:

depth

Hints on Tackling This Assignment:

Set depth as the y position for instances, with origin bottom center, to allow player to walk behind and in front of other instances.

287. Party Mechanics

Difficulty 4/5

Project Outline:

To create a system that allows the player to switch between two characters. Include a camera that follows the selected character.

Useful Functions and Built-in Variables:

point_distance
move_towards_point
keyboard_check_pressed

Hints on Tackling This Assignment:

Allow keys 1 2 3 to select player character. Create an instance that moves to selected character, set the camera to follow this instance.

GAMEMAKER PROGRAMMING CHALLENGES

Difficulty
4/5

288. Card Battle

Project Outline:

Create a card system based on characters with random stats. Allow the player to choose a stat and compare to computer's card, if player stat is bigger, then player wins

Useful Functions and Built-in Variables:

keyboard_check_pressed
alarm
ds_list_add
ds_list_shuffle

Hints on Tackling This Assignment:

Populate a 2D array with random stats. Show the player stats. Player then chooses one stat to compete against computer. The higher value wins.

289. Text Explode

Difficulty 3/5

Project Outline:

To take a string, and make shrink then explode as separate letters.

Useful Functions and Built-in Variables:

```
string_length
array_create
string_char_at
instance_create_layer
direction
speed
```

Hints on Tackling This Assignment:

Create a variable with a message. On mouse press shrink the text, then explode by taking each letter and send to an instance that draws and moves from center.

290. Branching Dialogue

Project Outline:

To create a dialogue system that adapts based on answers to asked questions.

Useful Functions and Built-in Variables:

draw_text

Hints on Tackling This Assignment:

Populate a 2D array with questions, options and numbers for what to do for each option. Display options, based on chosen option, display a new option and/or perform a task.

291. Marquee Text

Difficulty 3/5

Project Outline:

To create some horizontally scrolling text.

Useful Functions and Built-in Variables:

string_length
string_copy
draw_text

Hints on Tackling This Assignment:

Create a string variable, and draw first 5 characters, on alarm, take first letter and move to end of string. Repeat.

GAMEMAKER PROGRAMMING CHALLENGES

Difficulty
4/5

292. Avatar Creator B

Project Outline:

To create an avatar designing system that allows the user to save their creation to an image file.

Useful Functions and Built-in Variables:

get_save_filename
file_text_open_read
screen_save_part
file_text_close
sprite_get_number

Hints on Tackling This Assignment:

Create buttons, each of which loops through available sprites. Create a button for a random selection. Allow user to save the face as a PNG on their computer.

293. Create Level From Text File

Difficulty 3/5

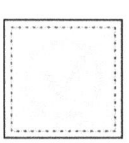

Project Outline:

Use data from a text file to create and position instances within a room.

Useful Functions and Built-in Variables:

file_text_*
while
string_length
for
string_char_at
instance_create_layer

Hints on Tackling This Assignment:

Read each line of a text file to an array. Then read each character and place an instance in the room based on line and position, for example @ for a player.

294. Enemy Shooting System

Project Outline:

To develop a system where an enemy increases its fire rate as it gets closer to the player.

Useful Functions and Built-in Variables:

alarm
distance_to_object

Hints on Tackling This Assignment:

Set a variable that increases as player gets closer to enemy. Use this value to set an alarm, which is used to create a projectile.

295. Dropping Effects

Difficulty 3/5

Project Outline:

To create a system that spawns instances above the room, which then fall down.

Useful Functions and Built-in Variables:

```
instance_create_layer
repeat
choose
irandom
effect_create_layer
```

Hints on Tackling This Assignment:

Create a line of effects that move from top to bottom of room. Choose a random effect, colour and size. Use built in effects.

296. Player Path

Difficulty 3/5

Project Outline:

To allow the player to add a series of points for a path, and then to move along it.

Useful Functions and Built-in Variables:

path_add
path_add_point
path_get_length
path_set_kind
draw_path

Hints on Tackling This Assignment:

Create a path, when user clicks mouse, add mouse position as a point on the path. Allow a key to toggle between straight and curved. Start path once it is has two positions.

Difficulty
3/5

297. Enemy Movement

Project Outline:

To create an enemy that periodically changes direction to move away from the player.

Useful Functions and Built-in Variables:

```
alarm
direction
point_direction
speed
```

Hints on Tackling This Assignment:

Set an enemy moving and set an alarm. On alarm set direction away from the player. Reset alarm.

298. Compass Points

Difficulty 4/5

Project Outline:

To draw angle between instances as points on a compass, for example: Northeast.

Useful Functions and Built-in Variables:

point_direction
return
round
case

Hints on Tackling This Assignment:

Get angle between player and enemy, send to a script that returns direction as text. Use another script to get angle and draw an indicator.

299. Drone Weapon

Difficulty 4/5

Project Outline:

To develop a weapon system that circles the player, but attacks an enemy if it gets too close.

Useful Functions and Built-in Variables:

`place_meeting`
`enum`
`instance_nearest`
`point_distance`
`move_towards_point`

Hints on Tackling This Assignment:

Create a drone that circles the player. When an enemy is in range, target the enemy. When enemy is destroyed, return to rotating around the player.

300. Old Film Effect

Difficulty 1/5

Project Outline:

To use GameMaker's built-in layer effects to make the game look like an old film.

Useful Functions and Built-in Variables:

No code.

Hints on Tackling This Assignment:

Set a room background tiled and moving horizontally. Add an effect layer to give an old film effect.

301. Weapon Recoil

Difficulty 3/5

Project Outline:

To make an alternative weapon recoil system.

Useful Functions and Built-in Variables:

enum
lengthdir_*
draw_sprite
draw_sprite_ext
sign

Hints on Tackling This Assignment:

Use a state machine to track the turrets actions, from active, move back and move forward. Prevent rotation if recoil is active.

Difficulty
2/5

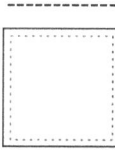

302. Change Cursor

Project Outline:

To use a different sprite based on player's current mouse input.

Useful Functions and Built-in Variables:

window_set_cursor
mouse_check_button
mouse_x mouse_y

Hints on Tackling This Assignment:

Use window_set_cursor to change the cursor based on interaction with an instance. For example, when over and when dragging to a new position.

303. Swap Music Tracks

Difficulty 3/5

Project Outline:

Switch between similar music tracks.

Useful Functions and Built-in Variables:

audio_play_sound
audio_sound_get_track_position
audio_sound_set_track_position
audio_stop_sound
mouse_wheel_*

Hints on Tackling This Assignment:

Allow mouse wheel to change between music tracks. Use audio_sound_* functions to get and set position of track, so they merge seamlessly.

304. Rotate Sprite With Off Center Origin

Difficulty 3/5

Project Outline:

To rotate a sprite when the origin is off center.

Useful Functions and Built-in Variables:

lengthdir_*
sprite_height
draw_sprite_ext

Hints on Tackling This Assignment:

Create an example where the sprite origin is bottom center. Calculate the position to rotate at, and use lengthdir_* functions to position the sprite.

305. Unlockable Buttons

Difficulty
3/5

Project Outline:

To create a set of buttons that appear when the player has reached a certain score, which can then be interacted with.

Useful Functions and Built-in Variables:

instance_create_layer
instance_exists
mouse_wheel_up

Hints on Tackling This Assignment:

Allow mouse wheel to increase player's score. When certain values are reached, create a button.

306. Follow Object With Avoidance

Difficulty 3/5

Project Outline:

To create an enemy that moves towards a player, whilst keeping a minimum distance and avoiding crates.

Useful Functions and Built-in Variables:

keyboard_check
instance_exists
distance_to_object
mp_potential_step
point_direction

Hints on Tackling This Assignment:

Use distance_to_object to calculate enemy distance to player. If above a range, step towards the player using mp_potential_step.

GAMEMAKER PROGRAMMING CHALLENGES

Difficulty
3/5

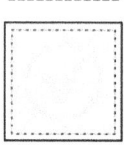

307. Circular Rotating Text A

Project Outline:

Draw characters from a string that rotate around a central Position.

Useful Functions and Built-in Variables:

string_length
for
string_char_at
lengthdir_*

Hints on Tackling This Assignment:

Create an array to hold the letters. Use a for loop and lengthdir_* functions to draw the text rotating around a central position.

308. Place Instances Without Blocking Path

Project Outline:

To create a system that only allows placement of blocks if they don't block a path from start and end points.

Useful Functions and Built-in Variables:

```
window_set_cursor
instance_create_layer
mp_grid_add_instances
mp_grid_clear_all
mp_grid_path
```

Hints on Tackling This Assignment:

Allow player to place blocks. Only allow placement if it does not block a path between start and end points. You can do this by placing an instance and checking path, if path is blocked remove it.

309. Shooting AI Helper

Difficulty 3/5

Project Outline:

To create a little helper that rotates around the player and shoots projectiles at enemies in range.

Useful Functions and Built-in Variables:

instance_nearest
point_distance
point_direction
lengthdir_*

Hints on Tackling This Assignment:

Rotate around the player using lengthdir_* functions. Periodically check for nearby enemy and create bullet targeting it if in range.

310. Do Something After Given Time

Difficulty
3/5

Project Outline:

To use a time source, rather than an alarm, to make something happen after a set time.

Useful Functions and Built-in Variables:

call_later
time_source_units_seconds
function

Hints on Tackling This Assignment:

Make a function and set a call to it using call_later.

311. Extending Frog Tongue Without Sprite

Difficulty 3/5

Project Outline:

To make a tongue that extends and retracts to given position.

Useful Functions and Built-in Variables:

enum
point_direction
point_distance
lengthdir_*
draw_line_width

Hints on Tackling This Assignment:

Save the mouse position when clicked. Use this position to calculate a distance and angle. Use a variable to move to this position by drawing a line.

312. Extending Frog Tongue With Sprite

Project Outline:

To draw an extending and retracting tongue using sprites.

Useful Functions and Built-in Variables:

```
enum
point_distance
point_direction
for
lengthdir_*
```

Hints on Tackling This Assignment:

To get distance and angle from start and end, and break down to series of points and draw a sprite at that position.

313. Sprite With Two Attack Modes

Difficulty 3/5

Project Outline:

To create a system where the player has two modes of attacks, each initiated by a different mouse button.

Useful Functions and Built-in Variables:

enum
mouse_check_button
sprite_index
image_index

Hints on Tackling This Assignment:

Use a state machine to track what the player is doing. Change sprite when attack starts. Use animation end event to set back to idle.

GAMEMAKER PROGRAMMING CHALLENGES

Difficulty
3/5

314. Rotating Tower With Subimages

Project Outline:

Use per-rendered 3D sprites that rotate. You can grab some tower sprites at: https://gamemaker.io/en/bundles

Useful Functions and Built-in Variables:

image_number
point_direction
image_index

Hints on Tackling This Assignment:

Calculate 360 divided by the number of subimages, use this value to determine which sprite to draw.

315. Rotate View and Instances

Difficulty 3/5

Project Outline:

To rotate the view and all instances within it.

Useful Functions and Built-in Variables:

```
view_camera
camera_set_view_angle
mouse_check_button
draw_sprite_ext
```

Hints on Tackling This Assignment:

Allow mouse buttons to increase and decrease a value. Use this value to rotate view and instances.

316. Reverse Sentence Order

Project Outline:

To extract words from a string and display in reverse order.

Useful Functions and Built-in Variables:

for
string_length
string_copy

Hints on Tackling This Assignment:

Split a string at spaces and save each word to an array. Loop through this array in reverse order and display.

317. Generate Random Sentence

Difficulty 3/5

Project Outline:

To randomly choose words to construct a sentence.

Useful Functions and Built-in Variables:

choose
draw_text

Hints on Tackling This Assignment:

Use choose to select random words for a sentence.
Then put them into a string and draw it.

GAMEMAKER PROGRAMMING CHALLENGES

Difficulty
3/5

318. Plane Height and Shadow

Project Outline:

To create a moveable plane that can also move up and down, and to draw a shadow of it that changes size based on height.

Useful Functions and Built-in Variables:

image_xscale
image_yscale
lengthdir_*
draw_sprite_ext

Hints on Tackling This Assignment:

Allow AD to move player's plane. WS to change the scale of the plane and its shadow.

319. Moon Lander AI

Difficulty 3/5

Project Outline:

To a make a moon ship that automatically lands on a platform.

Useful Functions and Built-in Variables:

hspeed
vspeed
random_range
place_meeting

Hints on Tackling This Assignment:

Move towards the target, by changing speed, with some variance. If on platform and speed is below a certain value, set as landed.

GAMEMAKER PROGRAMMING CHALLENGES

Difficulty
3/5

320. Player Character Selection B

Project Outline:

To allow the player to select a character using WSAD.

Useful Functions and Built-in Variables:

draw_roundrect
draw_set_colour
keyboard_check_pressed

Hints on Tackling This Assignment:

Allow WSAD to change selection. Draw a rectangle around selected character.

Difficulty
2/5

321. Slowly Reduce Health

Project Outline:

To slowly reduce a player's health when damaged.

Useful Functions and Built-in Variables:

draw_sprite
draw_sprite_ext
sprite_get_width

Hints on Tackling This Assignment:

Slowly reduce health to a target value when damage is taken.

GAMEMAKER PROGRAMMING CHALLENGES

Difficulty
3/5

322. Level Progress - 2 Players

Project Outline:

Display a progress meter to show progress of 2 players.

Useful Functions and Built-in Variables:

clamp
draw_line_width
draw_sprite
mouse_check_button

Hints on Tackling This Assignment:

Move the player with mouse button. Draw two sprites on a bar, relative to their progress on the level.

323. Find Random Position Outside View

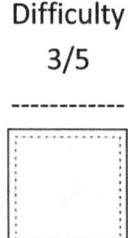

Difficulty
3/5

Project Outline:

Select an instance at a position outside the current view.

Useful Functions and Built-in Variables:

camera_get_view_*
point_in_rectangle
irandom

Hints on Tackling This Assignment:

Make a script that returns whether a position is inside the current view. If it is, choose a random position until outside the view.

GAMEMAKER PROGRAMMING CHALLENGES

Difficulty
3/5

324. Recolour Sprite With Blendmode

Project Outline:

To change the colour of an image using blendmode.

Useful Functions and Built-in Variables:

surface_exists
surface_create
surface_set_target
gpu_set_blendmode
draw_surface

Hints on Tackling This Assignment:

Create a surface, and set colour using a random value with draw_clear_alpha. Set the gpu blendmode with bm_add, draw the instance on the surface, then reset the blendmode with bm_normal and draw surface.

Difficulty
3/5

325. Draw Text With Flashing Border

Project Outline:

To draw text with flashing border that changes colours.

Useful Functions and Built-in Variables:

enum
alarm
for
draw_set_colour
draw_text

Hints on Tackling This Assignment:

Draw text using a for loop to change positions to give a border. Change the border size between two values to make it flash in and out.

Difficulty
3/5

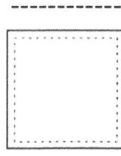

326. Count Down Text

Project Outline:

To queue and display a series of messages.

Useful Functions and Built-in Variables:

```
instance_destroy
if
draw_set_alpha
draw_text_transformed
ds_list_delete
ds_list_size
```

Hints on Tackling This Assignment:

Add a series of strings to ds_list. Take the first entry and display. Then delete first entry and grab the next entry. Destroy when no more strings to show.

327. Showing Damage To Spaceship

Difficulty 3/5

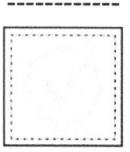

Project Outline:

Create a smokeeffect that increases as the enemy takes damage.

Useful Functions and Built-in Variables:

health
instance_create_layer
draw_sprite_ext

Hints on Tackling This Assignment:

Allow mouse wheel to reduce health. As health decreases use instance_create_layer to reate more instances of a smoke effect to show more damage.

Difficulty 3/5

328. Change Volume Of Music

Project Outline:

To allow user to change the volume.

Useful Functions and Built-in Variables:

```
audio_play_sound
audio_sound_gain
clamp
```

Hints on Tackling This Assignment:

Start playing music and assign to a variable. Use another variable to keep track of and change volume. Adjust playing volume with audio_sound_gain.

Difficulty
3/5

329. Slide In Out Stats

Project Outline:

Allow a player to click a button to move stats in and out.

Useful Functions and Built-in Variables:

xstart
ystart

Hints on Tackling This Assignment:

Allow player to click a box and set a flag to true or false. Move to a target position or move back based on the flag.

Difficulty
3/5

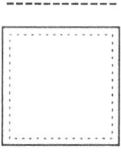

330. Expanding Rotating Fire Effect

Project Outline:

To create a fire effect that expands from a spawning point, whilst increasing in size.

Useful Functions and Built-in Variables:

for
instance_create_layer
lengthdir_*
draw_sprite_ext

Hints on Tackling This Assignment:

Move out from a starting position, using lengthdir_* to increase angle and distance. Also increase image scale by small amount each frame.

GAMEMAKER PROGRAMMING CHALLENGES

Difficulty
3/5

331. Move To Position On Sine Wave

Project Outline:

Use a sine wave to move an instance on its y axis whilst moving horizontally.

Useful Functions and Built-in Variables:

```
sin
current_time
```

Hints on Tackling This Assignment:

Move an instance on the x axis. Change the y position using a sine function.

332. Recoil When Shooting

Difficulty 3/5

Project Outline:

Allow a player to move in four directions and fire a bullet. Recoil the player when it shoots.

Useful Functions and Built-in Variables:

```
lengthdir_*
direction
image_angle
enum
```

Hints on Tackling This Assignment:

Use an enum to up player states, when recoiling move away from bullet direction, then return.

333. Hold Button To Jump Higher

Difficulty 3/5

Project Outline:

To allow the player to jump higher whilst a button is held down.

Useful Functions and Built-in Variables:

vspeed
gravity
instance_position
keyboard_check_released
keyboard_check

Hints on Tackling This Assignment:

Detect when a key is pressed, then add to movement to continue moving up until key is released.

GAMEMAKER PROGRAMMING CHALLENGES

Difficulty
2/5

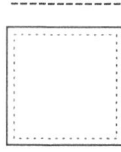

334. Choose Random Number

Project Outline:

To choose a random value within a given range using a button

Useful Functions and Built-in Variables:

point_in_rectangle
mouse_check_button_*
irandom_range
bbox_*

Hints on Tackling This Assignment:

Use point_in_rectangle and mouse_check_button_* to detect a press over a button. Use irandom_range to select a random number. Draw the value of this number.

335. Iris Effect Room Transition

Difficulty 3/5

Project Outline:

To draw a room transition effect of a growing and shrinking circle.

Useful Functions and Built-in Variables:

room_width
room_height
draw_circle
for

Hints on Tackling This Assignment:

Use a changing variable to draw a series of circles using a for loop.

336. Only Show Visible Walls

Project Outline:

To create a system that only makes walls appear if the player has a direct line of site.

Useful Functions and Built-in Variables:

collision_line
draw_line
if

Hints on Tackling This Assignment:

Use collision_line to set a flag to true or false whether the player can see A wall. Draw the wall if flag is true.

Difficulty
3/5

337. Four Directional Dash

Project Outline:

To create a system that allows the player to dash in four directions.

Useful Functions and Built-in Variables:

switch
case
position_meeting

Hints on Tackling This Assignment:

Set a countdown when dash starts, and a flag. If flag is true move in the direction player is facing, checking for collision.

GAMEMAKER PROGRAMMING CHALLENGES

Difficulty
3/5

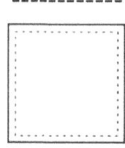

338. Rectangle Room Transition Effect

Project Outline:

Draw a growing and shrinking rectangle to create a room transition.

Useful Functions and Built-in Variables:

draw_rectangle
for

Hints on Tackling This Assignment:

Use a variable to keep track of size and increase / decrease. Use this value with a for loop to draw a series of rectangles.

Difficulty
2/5

339. Eight Directional Movement B

Project Outline:

To allow the player to move in eight directions.

Useful Functions and Built-in Variables:

keyboard_check
image_speed
sprite_index

Hints on Tackling This Assignment:

Check for keypress or multiple keypresses, and update the x and y positions accordingly.

340. Segmented Neck

Difficulty 3/5

Project Outline:

To draw a segmented neck from instance to mouse position, using a preset number of segments.

Useful Functions and Built-in Variables:

mouse_x
mouse_y
for
lengthdir_*
mouse_check_button
draw_sprite

Hints on Tackling This Assignment:

Divide the distance between body and mouse position by number of segments. Use a for loop and lengthdir_* function to calculate the position based on angle to mouse position.

341. Hold To Change Sprite

Difficulty 3/5

Project Outline:

To change a sprite when the mouse button is held down over it.

Useful Functions and Built-in Variables:

mouse_check_button
position_meeting
mouse_check_button_*
draw_sprite_ext

Hints on Tackling This Assignment:

Use a variable that counts how long mouse button is held down over an instance. When a target is met, set a flag to true. Draw according to this flag.

Difficulty
3/5

342. Piece Movement

Project Outline:

Create a system to move pieces around a board.

Useful Functions and Built-in Variables:

position_meeting
mouse_check_button_*
instance_place
move_snap

Hints on Tackling This Assignment:

Select a piece when clicked, move around with mouse position with move_snap. Place in position when released, deleting other piece if present.

343. Enemy With Trailing Instances

Project Outline:

Make some instances that follow another.

Useful Functions and Built-in Variables:

sin
room_width

Hints on Tackling This Assignment:

Set some instance to move between horizontal borders. Use varying values with a sine wave to make them follow each other.

Difficulty 3/5

344. Reverse Controls

Project Outline:

Allow WSAD to move player. Reverse controls upon mouse button presses.

Useful Functions and Built-in Variables:

mouse_check_button_*
keyboard_check
clamp

Hints on Tackling This Assignment:

Allow the player to move using WSAD, keeping in room with clamp. Allow mouse buttons to reverse / reset controls. Use a flag to determine whether normal or reversed controls.

Difficulty 3/5

345. Four Direction Enemy

Project Outline:

Make an enemy point in direction when moving along a path.

Useful Functions and Built-in Variables:

```
mp_grid_*
path_start
instance_create_layer
direction
```

Hints on Tackling This Assignment:

Create a path between current position and target with no diagonals, avoiding instances. Start moving on path. Get direction and set sprite for that direction, so it points in the direction it is walking.

346. Four Direction Move To Mouse

Project Outline:

To move towards mouse. Using sprite that matches direction moving.

Useful Functions and Built-in Variables:

switch
case
point_direction
sprite_index
mouse_check_button

Hints on Tackling This Assignment:

Calculate nearest 90 degree angle to mouse. Use a switch statement to set sprite and move.

347. Draw Sprite Border

Difficulty 3/5

Project Outline:

Draw a border around a sprite using gpu_set_fog.

Useful Functions and Built-in Variables:

gpu_set_fog
draw_sprite_ext
instance_position

Hints on Tackling This Assignment:

Draw a border by setting gpu_set_fog. Use a for loop to draw sprite at different positions. Turn off fog and draw sprite. Only do this when mouse is over it.

Difficulty
3/5

348. Keep Crosshair In View

Project Outline:

To prevent a crosshair from leaving the current view.

Useful Functions and Built-in Variables:

camera_get_view_*
clamp

Hints on Tackling This Assignment:

Get the current view position, along with view width and height. Use clamp to keep a crosshair within the view region.

349. Safe Password Code

Difficulty 3/5

Project Outline:

To draw a keypad and allow user to enter a code. Correct code opens the safe.

Useful Functions and Built-in Variables:

position_meeting
string_length
mouse_check_button_*

Hints on Tackling This Assignment:

Create a button for each digit, add to a global value when clicked. Use another button to enter and check the code, opening the safe if correct. Also add a button to clear current combination guess.

350. Morph Between Images

Difficulty
5/5

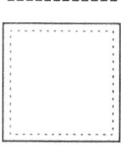

Project Outline:

Gradually morph between two images, using mouse button input.

Useful Functions and Built-in Variables:

surface_create
surface_exists
surface_set_target
gpu_set_*

Hints on Tackling This Assignment:

Morph and blend between two surfaces and blend_modes to create a transition effect.

351. Rotate Sprite Randomly

Difficulty 3/5

Project Outline:

To rotate a sprite with some randomness when mouse button is clicked over it.

Useful Functions and Built-in Variables:

choose
alarm

Hints on Tackling This Assignment:

When an instance is clicked, set a flag to rotate.
Use flag to rotate instance. Reset start angle when alarm triggers.

352. Rotating Stars Effect

Project Outline:

To create an expanding rotating star effect.

Useful Functions and Built-in Variables:

```
repeat
instance_create_layer
lengthdir_*
draw_sprite_ext
```

Hints on Tackling This Assignment:

On mouse click spawn 36 stars, each with a different angle. Gradually move away from spawn position and fade image.

353. Fade In Out Messages

Project Outline:

To display a sequence of messages, that fade in and out.

Useful Functions and Built-in Variables:

draw_set_alpha
draw_text
array_length

Hints on Tackling This Assignment:

Populate an array with messages. Fade the first message in and out, then move to next message. Repeat until all messages have been shown.

Difficulty
3/5

354. Pick Up and Carry

Project Outline:

To make a system that allows the player to pick up an item, walk with it and place it back down.

Useful Functions and Built-in Variables:

keyboard_check_pressed

Hints on Tackling This Assignment:

Set a global flag to determine if an instance is held or not. Set a key to pickup or put-down. When held, make collected item move with the player.

Difficulty
3/5

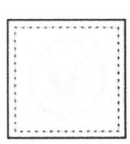

355. Bouncing Text Effect

Project Outline:

To display some text that bounces up and down.

Useful Functions and Built-in Variables:

array_length
mouse_check_button

Hints on Tackling This Assignment:

Queue messages within an array. Take message and bounce up and down by changing y position then select next message. Destroy when all have been shown.

GAMEMAKER PROGRAMMING CHALLENGES

Difficulty
3/5

356. Motion Blur With Movement

Project Outline:

To a motion blur trail effect when an instance moves.

Useful Functions and Built-in Variables:

ds_list_create
ds_list_size
ds_list_delete
alarm for
ds_list_add

Hints on Tackling This Assignment:

Create two ds_lists to hold x y positions. Set a short repeating alarm to add current position. Keep list at a max size. Use a for loop to draw at locations, with alpha.

357. Draw Sprite To Wall Edge

Project Outline:

To crop part of a sprite when it overlaps a wall.

Useful Functions and Built-in Variables:

bbox_left
bboxx_right
sprite_width
draw_sprite_part
other

Hints on Tackling This Assignment:

Detect if player sprite overlaps another instance. If it does don't draw that part of the sprite, by using draw_sprite_part.

GAMEMAKER PROGRAMMING CHALLENGES

Difficulty
3/5

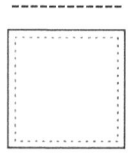

358. Create and Detonate Bomb With Same Button

Project Outline:

To allow the player to place and detonate a bomb with the same mouse button.

Useful Functions and Built-in Variables:

instance_create_layer
draw_rectangle
for

Hints on Tackling This Assignment:

On keypress create an instance of a bomb (it no bomb currently existing). On second keypess detenote it.

359. Rotatable 3D Car

Difficulty 3/5

Project Outline:

To allow a car to rotate 360' using a collection of per-rendered sprites.

Useful Functions and Built-in Variables:

image_speed
image_index
motion_set

Hints on Tackling This Assignment:

Allow player to use AD to rotate a car by changing the image_index. Use motion_set to move in current direction using basic math.

360. Rotatable Ship With Multiple Weapons

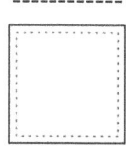

Project Outline:

To create a ship with weapon placements that rotate with the ship and fire projectiles.

Useful Functions and Built-in Variables:

draw_sprite_ext
lengthdir_*
alarm

Hints on Tackling This Assignment:

Create a movable ship, with 3 weapons. Use lengthdir_* to keep weapons in place as the ship rotates. Use an alarm to spawn bullets at each weapon position.

**Difficulty
1/5**

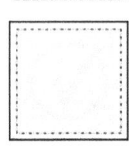

361. Draw Text With Shadow

Project Outline:

To draw text with a drop shadow.

Useful Functions and Built-in Variables:

draw_set_colour
draw_text

Hints on Tackling This Assignment:

Draw text with colour at an offset, then draw over it with another colour without offset.

362. Attacking With Custom Hit Box

Project Outline:

Create an instance for collision detection when a player attacks. Provide multiple attacks.

Useful Functions and Built-in Variables:

alarm
sprite_index
image_index
instance_create_layer

Hints on Tackling This Assignment:

Allow player to use keys to perform a number of attacks. During attack create an instance that could be used to detect a collision with an enemy.

363. Draw Healthbar From Two Sprites

Difficulty 3/5

Project Outline:

To draw a healthbar using two overlapping sprites.

Useful Functions and Built-in Variables:

health
clamp
draw_sprite
draw_sprite_part

Hints on Tackling This Assignment:

Allow user to change health value. Draw sprite for background, then use draw_sprite_part to overlay it based on value of health.

Difficulty 3/5

364. Save Players Stats

Project Outline:

To allow a player to save their stats in a text file at a location of their choice.

Useful Functions and Built-in Variables:

```
get_save_filename
file_text_open_write
file_text_write_string
file_text_writeln
```

Hints on Tackling This Assignment:

Generate some random data for testing. Allow user to set a name and location for a file. Create file, write data and then close it.

365. Circular Rotating Text B

Project Outline:

To draw characters from text that rotate a central point.

Useful Functions and Built-in Variables:

for
string_char_at
lengthdir_*
draw_text_ext_transformed

Hints on Tackling This Assignment:

Take each letter from a string and add to an array.
Use a for loop to go through each letter at an angle.
Increase the angle each step to make letters rotate.

366. Spiralling Weapon

Difficulty 3/5

Project Outline:

To make a weapon that circles an enemy, gradually getting closer.

Useful Functions and Built-in Variables:

```
enum
distance_to_object
distance_to_point
lengthdir_*
move_towards_point
```

Hints on Tackling This Assignment:

Spawn a weapon that moves to target. When within a range start spiraling around it, gradually getting closer. When colliding with target, reduce target's HP.

367. Selectable Characters

Difficulty 3/5

Project Outline:

To display a set of characters with pre-determined stats that the player can select from.

Useful Functions and Built-in Variables:

draw_sprite_ext
draw_set_color
draw_rectangle

Hints on Tackling This Assignment:

Create several player objects, with a parent assigned. Use parent to visually show when it is selected by drawing a rectangle around it. When clicked, deselect any other.

GAMEMAKER PROGRAMMING CHALLENGES

Difficulty
4/5

368. Proximity Helper

Project Outline:

Spawn a helper when near an instance, that the player can control with the mouse and interact with the instance, hovering over it to provide info

Useful Functions and Built-in Variables:

window_set_cursor
place_meeting
draw_sprite
instance_nearest
distance_to_point
draw_text

Hints on Tackling This Assignment:

When player is within a range of an instance, show a hand icon That can be moved with mouse, when over an instance, use draw_text to draw some info.

Difficulty
4/5

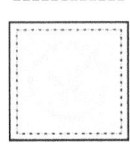

369. Temporary Invincibility

Project Outline:

To allow the player to turn on temporary invincibility.

Useful Functions and Built-in Variables:

lengthdir_*
draw_line_width
for
position_meeting

Hints on Tackling This Assignment:

When clicked set invincibility to 100 and slowly reduce. Draw a circular bar to show current value. By drawing lines with colour based on direction and value.

370. Falling Crates

Project Outline:

To create boulders that fall down, left or right if there is a free space to fall in to.

Useful Functions and Built-in Variables:

enum
place_meeting
move_towards_point
point_distance

Hints on Tackling This Assignment:

Allow user to click a crate to remove it. If space below, drop down. Otherwise look for a space below at both left and right. Move into empty space if there is one.

GAMEMAKER PROGRAMMING CHALLENGES

Difficulty
3/5

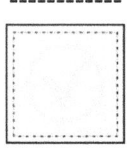

371. Countdown Clock

Project Outline:

To create a clock dial with a hand that counts down.

Useful Functions and Built-in Variables:

draw_sprite_ext
draw_sprite

Hints on Tackling This Assignment:

Draw a clock face and a hand that slowly moves as a variable counts down.

GAMEMAKER PROGRAMMING CHALLENGES

Difficulty
4/5

372. Rings Fly Through

Project Outline:

To allow a player to fly inside a ring, showing the back part behind the player and the front over the player.

Useful Functions and Built-in Variables:

```
instance_place
draw_sprite
draw_sprite_ext
draw_rectangle
```

Hints on Tackling This Assignment:

Create a hoop, with a small collision box so it can detect if player is in middle. If it is draw player between front and back sprites. If not, draw behind.

Difficulty
3/5

373. Text Based Menu

Project Outline:

To create a text based menu that allows user to change and select options.

Useful Functions and Built-in Variables:

array_length for
draw_set_font
draw_text
mouse_check_button
keyboard_check_pressed

Hints on Tackling This Assignment:

Use array to store all options as strings, and an array for target rooms. Use a for loop to draw all options, changing font and colour if currently selected.

Difficulty
3/5

374. Charge Jump

Project Outline:

To increase a jump height the longer a mouse button is held down. Charge whilst held down and jump upon release.

Useful Functions and Built-in Variables:

```
mouse_check_button_*
vspeed
gravity
```

Hints on Tackling This Assignment:

Start an increasing variable when mouse button is pressed, adding to it whilst it is held down. Upon button released set -vspeed to make instance jump.

375. Proximity Cone Of Vision

Difficulty 4/5

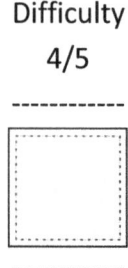

Project Outline:

Create a sweeping cone of vision that detects if it can see the player.

Useful Functions and Built-in Variables:

image_angle
distance_to_point
collision_triangle

Hints on Tackling This Assignment:

Create a rotating enemy that also has a triangle that sweep around with it Detect if the player is within the triangle, Change a flag accordingly.

376. Instance Selector

Difficulty 2/5

Project Outline:

To allow user to click select an instance, deselecting previously selected.

Useful Functions and Built-in Variables:

image_index
irandom

Hints on Tackling This Assignment:

Make an instance choose a random subimage. When clicked set to selected and draw a circle over it, deselecting any other. Right button to deselect.

377. Instance Placer

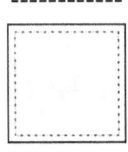

Difficulty 3/5

Project Outline:

To randomly place instances at previously determined positions.

Useful Functions and Built-in Variables:

instance_find
instance_exists
instance_number
sprite_get_number
irandom

Hints on Tackling This Assignment:

Place a number of instances for spawn points in the room. Place another instance at one of these positions at random.

378. Loot Dropper

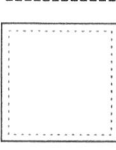

Project Outline:

To create a character that moves and periodically drops items.

Useful Functions and Built-in Variables:

path_start
alarm
image_angle
direction
instance_create_layer

Hints on Tackling This Assignment:

Start an enemy on a path that loops. Use an alarm to periodically create a gem instance.

379. Draw Decimal Fraction

Difficulty 3/5

Project Outline:

To draw and format a decimal to a given number of positions.

Useful Functions and Built-in Variables:

```
random
mouse_check_button_*
string_format
```

Hints on Tackling This Assignment:

Generate a random number. Allow player to choose how many decimals to show. Format and draw.

380. Stats With Buttons

Project Outline:

To allow the player to view stats by clicking a buttons.

Useful Functions and Built-in Variables:

position_meeting
mouse_check_button_*
draw_text

Hints on Tackling This Assignment:

Set up some buttons that can be clicked.
Use draw_text to draw info for that button's stat.

**Difficulty
4/5**

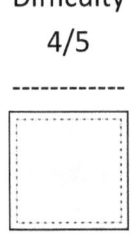

381. Show Parts Of A Sentence

Project Outline:

To break a string down into words and allow user to select how many words to display.

Useful Functions and Built-in Variables:

string_length
string_copy
clamp
for

Hints on Tackling This Assignment:

Split a string into words stored in an array. Use a variable that the user can change to draw a set number of words.

382. Weapon Reload System

Difficulty 3/5

Project Outline:

To create a weapon with a magazine that empties so the player has to reload, playing a voice to notify the player.

Useful Functions and Built-in Variables:

audio_play_sound
choose
instance_create_layer

Hints on Tackling This Assignment:

Use a variable to keep track of player's ammo. If player tries to shoot with no ammo, play a short voice message at random to indicate no ammo. Allow right mouse button to reload.

Difficulty
1/5

383. Moving Eyes

Project Outline:

To create some eyes that follow the direction of the mouse cursor.

Useful Functions and Built-in Variables:

```
image_angle
point_direction
```

Hints on Tackling This Assignment:

Rotate the sprite by setting image_angle to direction of the mouse cursor.

Difficulty
1/5

384. Audio Control

Project Outline:

To create a system that stops a playing sound effect when another plays.

Useful Functions and Built-in Variables:

audio_play_sound
audio_is_playing
audio_stop_sound

Hints on Tackling This Assignment:

Stop any playing audio with audio_stop_sound before playing another effect.

Difficulty
3/5

385. Prevent Mouse Cursor Moving Over Instance

Project Outline:

To make a system that prevents the mouse cursor from going over certain instances.

Useful Functions and Built-in Variables:

mouse_y
mouse_x
mouse_check_button
window_set_cursor
position_meeting

Hints on Tackling This Assignment:

Use some variables to store last mouse position when not over a crate. Disable cursor and draw a custom sprite at that position when over a crate.

Difficulty
5/5

386. Directional Shadow

Project Outline:

To create a shadow that moves depending on light source.

Useful Functions and Built-in Variables:

surface_set_target
with
lengthdir_*
sprite_exists
point_direction
draw_sprite_ext
surface_reset_target
draw_surface_ext

Hints on Tackling This Assignment:

Loop through all instances and get direction from light source to instance. Draw the shadows on a surface and then draw the surface with reduced alpha.

387. Scale Image

Difficulty 2/5

Project Outline:

To scale an image based on distance from the mouse position.

Useful Functions and Built-in Variables:

mouse_x
mouse_y
sprite_width
sprite_height
draw_sprite_ext

Hints on Tackling This Assignment:

Calculate the scale of the image based on position of sprite origin to mouse position. Draw sprite with those scale settings with draw_sprite_ext.

GAMEMAKER PROGRAMMING CHALLENGES

Difficulty
1/5

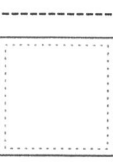

388. Draw Bounding Box

Project Outline:

To draw the bounding box for any given instance.

Useful Functions and Built-in Variables:

draw_rectangle
bbox_left
bbox_top
bbox_right
bbox_bottom

Hints on Tackling This Assignment:

Just draw a rectangle using the coordinates of the bounding box.

389. Poker Hand

Difficulty 4/5

Project Outline:

To shuffle a deck of cards and deal 5 cards, and sort by suit and value

Useful Functions and Built-in Variables:

ds_list_create
ds_list_add
ds_list_shuffle
ds_list_delete
sprite_get_name
ds_list_sort

Hints on Tackling This Assignment:

Create a list and add all cards as sprites. Shuffle and take top 5 cards for player hand. Use ds_list_sort to sort by suit and value. Use sprite name to get suit and value. Draw as sprite and text.

GAMEMAKER PROGRAMMING CHALLENGES

Difficulty
4/5

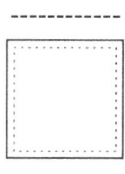

390. Choose and Name Random Playing Card

Project Outline:

To shuffle a deck of cards and deal one, showing it visually with a text description.

Useful Functions and Built-in Variables:

ds_list_create
ds_list_add
ds_list_shuffle
ds_list_delete
sprite_get_name

Hints on Tackling This Assignment:

Create a list and add all cards as sprites. Shuffle and take the top cards for player hand. Use sprite name to get suit and value. Draw as sprite and text.

Difficulty
1/5

391. Fade Sprite In and Out

Project Outline:

To gradually fade two images in and out in a cycle.

Useful Functions and Built-in Variables:

mouse_check_button
clamp
draw_sprite_ext

Hints on Tackling This Assignment:

Use a variable that changes between 0 and 1 based on mouse button input. Draw sprite with alpha of this value.

392. Circular Healthbar That Adjusts

Project Outline:

To create a circular healthbar that automatically adapts to the size of the instance's sprite.

Useful Functions and Built-in Variables:

```
clamp
sprite_width
lengthdir_*
draw_line_width
for
```

Hints on Tackling This Assignment:

Get the width of the instance's sprite and use this value to calculate a radius and thickness of the bar. Use lengthdir_* to draw a series of lines.

393. Dropping Block

Difficulty 3/5

Project Outline:

To allow blocks to fall down if there is space below them.

Useful Functions and Built-in Variables:

```
mouse_check_button_*
instance_destroy
instance_position
place_meeting
```

Hints on Tackling This Assignment:

Remove a block when clicked with mouse. Check for empty space below a block, if there is move down until it hits another block or floor.

GAMEMAKER PROGRAMMING CHALLENGES

Difficulty
3/5

394. Slider

Project Outline:

To make a paddle that moves left and right with increasing speed whilst button is held down, then gradually slows down.

Useful Functions and Built-in Variables:

mouse_check_button
clamp

Hints on Tackling This Assignment:

Create a variable for speed. Allow player to move left and right with mouse buttons. Increase variable as button is held down to increase speed. Reduce speed each step to simulate friction.

GAMEMAKER PROGRAMMING CHALLENGES

Difficulty
3/5

395. Move To An Instance's Position

Project Outline:

To create a path based system that moves an instance to a random position and repeats, whilst avoiding instances.

Useful Functions and Built-in Variables:

instance_find
mouse_check_button
instance_exists
mp_grid_*
direction
image_angle

Hints on Tackling This Assignment:

To make character randomly choose an instance as a target. Use mp_grid to set up a grid and no go areas. Move character along path to the target.

396. Parachute Falling With Wobble

Difficulty 1/5

Project Outline:

To create a parachute that falls, with a bit of side-to-side wobbling.

Useful Functions and Built-in Variables:

`image_angle`

Hints on Tackling This Assignment:

Use a variable for angle of the sprite. Move this between -45 and 45 degrees.

397. Increasing Difficulty

Difficulty 2/5

Project Outline:

To create an enemy system so that when an enemy is killed, the next enemy's hp becomes stronger.

Useful Functions and Built-in Variables:

```
irandom_range
mouse_check_button_*
instance_create_layer
instance_destroy
```

Hints on Tackling This Assignment:

Use a global variable for enemy hp that increases each time an enemy is destroyed. When destroyed create a new enemy at a random position and set new hp value.

398. Incoming Enemy

Project Outline:

To create a system that alerts the player when a new enemy is on the way by playing an alert sound.

Useful Functions and Built-in Variables:

choose
audio_play_sound
hspeed

Hints on Tackling This Assignment:

When an enemy is created off screen play a random alert sound. Move enemy across the screen.

399. Warp Portal

Difficulty 4/5

Project Outline:

To warp a player between two locations. Make the player shrink and then grow when warping.

Useful Functions and Built-in Variables:

enum
instance_position
move_towards_point
image_xscale
image_yscale

Hints on Tackling This Assignment:

When player collides with portal move it towards its center. Reduce image scale, when 0 move to other portal and increase scale.

Difficulty
3/5

400. Programable Characters

Project Outline:

To allow a player select a player to select and give it a task to perform.

Useful Functions and Built-in Variables:

```
position_meeting
point_direction
instance_position
```

Hints on Tackling This Assignment:

Set up a state machine for player with all the tasks it can do. When a character is clicked, store its id. When an action button is pressed, send a task to the player.

401. Drawing Sprite Fonts In Different Colours

Difficulty
3/5

Project Outline:

To use sprite fonts to create variable coloured letters from strings.

Useful Functions and Built-in Variables:

font_add_sprite_ext
string_length
font_get_size
string_char_at
string_upper

Hints on Tackling This Assignment:

Create two sprite based fonts in different colours. Loop through each character and set font based on upper or lower case. Draw character at correct position.

GAMEMAKER PROGRAMMING CHALLENGES

Difficulty
3/5

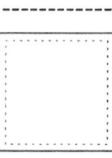

402. Stealth Zones

Project Outline:

To monitor a player's speed through an area, setting off an alarm sound if they move too fast.

Useful Functions and Built-in Variables:

keyboard_check
clamp
place_meeting
audio_play_sound

Hints on Tackling This Assignment:

Check if colliding with an instance, and check the players speed, setting off an audible alarm if moving too fast.

403. Dynamic Shadows

Project Outline:

To make directional shadows, based on the Sun's position.

Useful Functions and Built-in Variables:

hspeed
lengthdir_*
surface_create
surface_set_target
draw_clear_alpha
draw_surface_ext

Hints on Tackling This Assignment:

Create a sun that moves back and forth at top of room. Use angle from sun to instances to draw shadows onto a surface, then draw the surface.

404. Proximity Mines

Difficulty 3/5

Project Outline:

To create mine weapons that detonate when a player gets too close.

Useful Functions and Built-in Variables:

distance_to_object
audio_play_sound
effect_create_layer
instance_destroy
draw_circle

Hints on Tackling This Assignment:

Create a bomb with a range variable, draw this as a circle. When player gets in range, play sound, create an effect and destroy it.

Difficulty
3/5

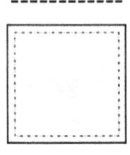

405. Sticky Projectiles

Project Outline:

Create a weapon that sticks to a surface and then detonates at end of a countdown.

Useful Functions and Built-in Variables:

image_angle
instance_create_layer
position_meeting
draw_healthbar

Hints on Tackling This Assignment:

Rotate a weapon to point to mouse position. On button press fire a bullet. When bullet collides with an object, stop moving and start a countdown to make it explode.

406. Reflecting Projectiles

Project Outline:

To create a weapon that bumps off of other instances.

Useful Functions and Built-in Variables:

```
image_angle
instance_create_layer
position_meeting
draw_healthbar
move_bounce_all
```

Hints on Tackling This Assignment:

Rotate a weapon to point to mouse position. On button press fire a bullet. When bullet collides with an object bounce off and start a countdown to make it explode.

407. Conveyor Belts

Difficulty 3/5

Project Outline:

To create a conveyor that moves a player when they stand on it.

Useful Functions and Built-in Variables:

keyboard_check
position_meeting

Hints on Tackling This Assignment:

Allow player to move with AD. When player is standing on a belt, make the player move in direction of belt by adding or subtracting from x position.

408. Spreading Fire

Difficulty 3/5

Project Outline:

To create burnable instances that spread fire to nearby instances.

Useful Functions and Built-in Variables:

mouse_check_button_*
instance_position
alarm
sprite_get_number
collision_circle_list

Hints on Tackling This Assignment:

When an instance is clicked change a flag to true to set on fire. Use an alarm to increase fire range. Set on fire any instances in range with collision_circle_list.

Difficulty 4/5

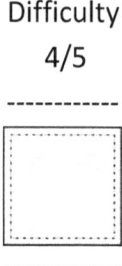

409. Boomerang Mechanic

Project Outline:

To create a player weapon that returns after being shot.

Useful Functions and Built-in Variables:

```
instance_create_layer
enum
move_towards_point
distance_to_point
distance_to_point
```

Hints on Tackling This Assignment:

Set up a state machine to control what the boomerang is doing. When launched move to target, then return back to the player.

GAMEMAKER PROGRAMMING CHALLENGES

Difficulty
2/5

410. Burnable Objects

Project Outline:

Create instances that the player can set light to and destroy.

Useful Functions and Built-in Variables:

alarm
room_speed
mouse_check_button_*

Hints on Tackling This Assignment:

When clicked, set a flag to start the fire. Use an alarm to increase fire size. When max size start reducing health and destroy when 0.

411. Echo Location

Difficulty 3/5

Project Outline:

To send out an expanding wave that shows instances.

Useful Functions and Built-in Variables:

ds_list_create
collision_circle_list
draw_circle
with

Hints on Tackling This Assignment:

Get instances in max range use collision_circle_list and add to a list. Repeat for min range and remove from list. Use to set flag that draws instances within range.

Difficulty
3/5

412. Smooth Dash Movement

Project Outline:

To create a dash system where player slowly speeds up to a maximum speed, then gradually slows down.

Useful Functions and Built-in Variables:

keyboard_check
enum

Hints on Tackling This Assignment:

Create a state machine to manage dashing. When dashing starts, change state and gradually increase speed in direction, after a count, slowly reduce speed.

Difficulty 3/5

413. Shock Wave

Project Outline:

To create an expanding shockwave that damages enemies as it goes.

Useful Functions and Built-in Variables:

```
ds_list_create
collision_circle_list
draw_circle
with
```

Hints on Tackling This Assignment:

Create an expanding wave with collision_circle_list (showing with draw_circle), that damages enemies.

414. Hover Mechanic

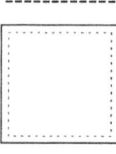

Project Outline:

To create a system that allows the player to temporally hover.

Useful Functions and Built-in Variables:

place_meeting
mouse_check_button
alarm

Hints on Tackling This Assignment:

Create a state machine to manage hovering. When active move up to a preset height, hover for a while and use an alarm trigger to move back down.

**Difficulty
3/5**

415. Jumping Pad

Project Outline:

To make jump upon collision with pad.

Useful Functions and Built-in Variables:

`instance_position`
`vspeed`

Hints on Tackling This Assignment:

When player walks on instance, make it jump by setting a negative vspeed.

GAMEMAKER PROGRAMMING CHALLENGES

Difficulty
2/5

416. Momentum Jumps

Project Outline:

Allow the player to jump higher when moving at faster horizontal speeds.

Useful Functions and Built-in Variables:

mouse_check_button_*
vspeed

Hints on Tackling This Assignment:

Use a variable for horizontal movement that increases as key is held down. Use that value to calculate jump speed when mouse button is pressed.

417. Gravity Flips

Difficulty 1/5

Project Outline:

Create a system that flips gravity for the player.

Useful Functions and Built-in Variables:

```
place_meeting
gravity
image_yscale
```

Hints on Tackling This Assignment:

Toggle a gravity direction with spacebar key. Change character yscale so it points in the direction of gravity.

Difficulty
1/5

418. Explosive Bombs

Project Outline:

A barrel that explodes upon collision with player.

Useful Functions and Built-in Variables:

```
instance_destroy
instance_create_layer
audio_play_sound
```

Hints on Tackling This Assignment:

When a player collides with a barrel, create an explosion instance with a sprite, play a sound and destroy barrel. Destroy explosion instance on last frame.

Difficulty
3/5

419. Explosive Barrels Chain

Project Outline:

Create explosive barrels that upon detonation set off other barrels within a range.

Useful Functions and Built-in Variables:

draw_circle
ds_list_create
collision_circle_list
for
ds_list_size

Hints on Tackling This Assignment:

When a barrel is clicked destroy it and create an explosion effect instances. When the effect animation ends create a list of barrels in range and destroy them.

Difficulty
3/5

420. End-of-Level Gate

Project Outline:

To spawn a level exit door once all instances have been collected.

Useful Functions and Built-in Variables:

instance_number
instance_create
instance_exists

Hints on Tackling This Assignment:

Use instance_exists to check if gem exists, if it doesn't spawn a door instance.

421. Coin Collection

Difficulty 3/5

Project Outline:

To make system that collects a coin when the player gets close to it.

Useful Functions and Built-in Variables:

```
distance_to_object
move_towards_point
instance_destroy
```

Hints on Tackling This Assignment:

Set a range variable for the coin. When the player is within this range, move towards player and destroy on collision.

422. One Way Blocks

Project Outline:

To create blocks that player can traverse in only one direction.

Useful Functions and Built-in Variables:

switch
case
mouse_check_button
instance_exists

Hints on Tackling This Assignment:

Set up an emum for blocks to set allowed direction. When player collides with block only allow movement if moving in direction of the block setting.

423. Wind

Difficulty 3/5

Project Outline:

Create a wind effect that applies movement upon to the player.

Useful Functions and Built-in Variables:

position_meeting

Hints on Tackling This Assignment:

When player collides with wind instance, add to the x position to make player move.

424. Nuke

Difficulty 4/5

Project Outline:

Create a weapon that kills all enemies within the current view.

Useful Functions and Built-in Variables:

```
camera_get_*
with
instance_create_layer
instance_destroy
audio_play_sound
```

Hints on Tackling This Assignment:

On input loop though all enemies and check if in current view. If they are, create an explosion effect and destroythem. Destroy explosion when animation ends.

425. Timed Collectibles

Difficulty 3/5

Project Outline:

Create collectibles that disappear if not promptly collected.

Useful Functions and Built-in Variables:

```
mouse_check_button_*
irandom
instance_create_layer
instance_destroy
draw_healthbar
```

Hints on Tackling This Assignment:

On mouse click spawn a coin at a random position. Use a variable for hp, that reduces each frame. When 0 destroy the coin. Show hp with a mini healthbar.

426. Retractable Bridge

Project Outline:

Create a system that allows for the extension and retraction of a bridge by using a lever.

Useful Functions and Built-in Variables:

```
sprite_width
mouse_check_button_*
with
position_meeting
```

Hints on Tackling This Assignment:

Set a switch that changes a flag when clicked, changing subimage on the value. Also send this value to a bridge to make it move left or right, within a range.

427. Tethering Mechanic

Difficulty 3/5

Project Outline:

Allow player to move a crate towards it.

Useful Functions and Built-in Variables:

```
instance_position
point_distance
point_direction
move_towards_point
draw_line
```

Hints on Tackling This Assignment:

Make a weapon rotate to mouse position. When mouse is over a crate, slowly move towards weapon, and draw a laser line from weapon to mouse position.

GAMEMAKER PROGRAMMING CHALLENGES

Difficulty
4/5

428. Squish Image

Project Outline:

To squish and squash an image.

Useful Functions and Built-in Variables:

image_xscale
image_yscale
random_range

Hints on Tackling This Assignment:

Gradually change an image's x and y scale to create a stretching and shrinking effect.

GAMEMAKER PROGRAMMING CHALLENGES

Difficulty
2/5

429. Adaptable Button

Project Outline:

To create a button that adapts to the size of text and current font.

Useful Functions and Built-in Variables:

image_speed
mouse_check_button
position_meeting
string_*
image_*scale

Hints on Tackling This Assignment:

Set image scale based on string width and height.
Draw this and then draw formatted text.

430. Star Effect

Project Outline:

To make space themed twinkling star effect.

Useful Functions and Built-in Variables:

repeat
irandom
instance_create_layer
alarm
choose
draw_sprite_ext

Hints on Tackling This Assignment:

Use repeat to place 200 stars at random. Use a random alarm to change colour and size of stars. Use draw_sprite_ext to draw with size and colour.

431. Cracked Walls

Difficulty 3/5

Project Outline:

Create wall instances that sustain damage if player runs into it whilst above a certain speed.

Useful Functions and Built-in Variables:

```
keyboard_check
mouse_check_button
clamp
place_meeting
instance_place
```

Hints on Tackling This Assignment:

Allow player to increase speed when holding a key down. When player collides with a wall above a speed value, damage the wall by changing image_index. Destroy wall when last frame is reached.

432. Pressure Plates

Project Outline:

Create a pressure plate that activates if the player stands on it for too long.

Useful Functions and Built-in Variables:

place_meeting
instance_create_layer
draw_healthbar

Hints on Tackling This Assignment:

Set a floor instance with hp. When player is on it reduce hp. When no hp drop an instance from above and set a flag. If not standing on increase hp to max, and reset flag.

Difficulty
3/5

433. Multiple Weapons

Project Outline:

To create a weapon system that fire multiple projectiles, each targeting a different enemy.

Useful Functions and Built-in Variables:

alarm
draw_rectangle
instance_create_layer
draw_healthbar
ds_list_*
ds_list_shuffle

Hints on Tackling This Assignment:

Make a weapon that fires 3 bullets. On creation make a list of all enemies and choose one at random that isn't already targeted.

GAMEMAKER PROGRAMMING CHALLENGES

Difficulty
3/5

434. Camera Pan

Project Outline:

To allow the user to examine the room by panning the camera.

Useful Functions and Built-in Variables:

keyboard_check
enum
sprite_height

Hints on Tackling This Assignment:

Set a view to follow an instance. Set this to player's position. Allow the camera to move with IKJL. When no keypress, slowly move back to the player.

435. Time-Locked Doors

Difficulty 3/5

Project Outline:

Create a door that opens and closes at specific times.

Useful Functions and Built-in Variables:

enum
draw_healthbar

Hints on Tackling This Assignment:

Set up a state machine for a door to move up, move down, wait up and wait down. Use a timer that changes state when triggered. Draw timer with a healthbar.

436. Momentum-Based Movement

Difficulty 3/5

Project Outline:

To make a player movement that carries some inertia after key is released.

Useful Functions and Built-in Variables:

motion_set
keyboard_check
speed

Hints on Tackling This Assignment:

Set player moving on a keypress with motion set.
Gradually slow down when no keypress by multiplying speed by a value slightly less than 1.

437. Laser Destruction Beam

Project Outline:

To create a laser that gradually eats away at an enemy sprite.

Useful Functions and Built-in Variables:

surface_create
surface_set_target
surface_reset_target
draw_line

Hints on Tackling This Assignment:

When a laser beam hits an enemy, remove part of its sprite to show damage.

Difficulty
4/5

438. Zoom Control

Project Outline:

To make a camera system that allows the player to zoom in and out.

Useful Functions and Built-in Variables:

camera_set_view_size
camera_set_view_angle
camera_set_view_pos
mouse_wheel_*
lerp

Hints on Tackling This Assignment:

Allow mouse wheel to zoom in and out. Use lerp to slowly change zoom to currently selected value. Use camera_set_* to set size, and position.

439. Teleport Pads

Difficulty 3/5

Teleports that move the player to a different location, and back again.

Project Outline:

To create a teleport system that moves players from one position in the room to another.

Useful Functions and Built-in Variables:

```
enum
keyboard_check
instance_place
place_meeting
```

Hints on Tackling This Assignment:

Use a state machine for managing teleportation. On collision with a teleport, fade out, reposition at target and fade in. Only allow again after leaving teleport.

GAMEMAKER PROGRAMMING CHALLENGES

Difficulty
3/5

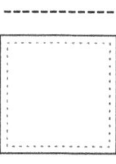

440. Customizable Turrets

Project Outline:

To allow user to move turrets that can be upgraded.

Useful Functions and Built-in Variables:

mouse_check_button_*
instance_position
mouse_wheel_*
move_snap

Hints on Tackling This Assignment:

Allow user to select a tower with mouse click. If held down move tower with mouse. Mouse wheel to change weapon. Click on empty space to deselect.

441. Direction Shield

Difficulty 3/5

Project Outline:

To develop a system that allows the player to make a shield in the current direction of travel.

Useful Functions and Built-in Variables:

keyboard_check
draw_sprite_ext

Hints on Tackling This Assignment:

Allow player to press M to activate a shield. Set position on the last direction player has moved. Draw relative to the player when active.

442. Enemy That Circles Player

Project Outline:

To create an enemy that circles and shoots at the player.

Useful Functions and Built-in Variables:

instance_create_layer
distance_to_point
move_towards_point
speed
alarm

Hints on Tackling This Assignment:

Create an enemy that moves towards player. When in a range, start circling the player and periodically fire a bullet towards the player.

GAMEMAKER PROGRAMMING CHALLENGES

Difficulty 4/5

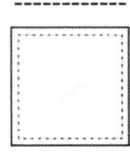

443. Target Enemy With Highest HP

Project Outline:

To create a weapon that targets an enemy with the highest hp.

Useful Functions and Built-in Variables:

```
alarm
instance_position
instance_create_layer
point_distance
move_towards_point
```

Hints on Tackling This Assignment:

Create a sight instance that targets an enemy with max hp, and moves towards it. Create a weapon that fires a bullet towards sight when sight is over the target.

444. Cloaking Device

Project Outline:

To allow the player to become invisible to enemies by means of a cloaking device.

Useful Functions and Built-in Variables:

```
keyboard_check
keyboard_check_pressed
clamp draw_sprite_ext
place_meeting
draw_healthbar
```

Hints on Tackling This Assignment:

Set a flag for cloaking that can be toggles with a keypress. When cloak is active draw with partial transparent and allow moving through enemy without damage.

445. Enemy Drops

Difficulty 2/5

Project Outline:

To make an enemy drop a collectible item when killed.

Useful Functions and Built-in Variables:

mouse_check_button_*
instance_destroy
instance_create_layer
sprite_get_number
irandom
image_speed

Hints on Tackling This Assignment:

Reduce an enemy's hp when clicked with mouse. When no hp, destroy and create a gem. Set gem to select a random subimage.

446. Rotating Obstacles

Difficulty 1/5

Project Outline:

Create a spinning obstacle that damages the player upon contact.

Useful Functions and Built-in Variables:

`image_angle`

Hints on Tackling This Assignment:

Make an instance rotate by adding to image_angle.

When player collides, reduce player's hp.

Difficulty 2/5

447. Enemy Patrol Patterns

Project Outline:

To set enemies moving along a predefined closed path. At end path restart again.

Useful Functions and Built-in Variables:

path_start
path_speed

Hints on Tackling This Assignment:

Set an instance to move on a path set in variable definitions. On mouse click, reverse path direction.

Difficulty
2/5

448. Sinking Sands

Project Outline:

To create a sand block that the player sinks into when standing on it.

Useful Functions and Built-in Variables:

keyboard_check
place_meeting

Hints on Tackling This Assignment:

When player is standing on sand, allow it to sink by increase y value. Allow pressing W to climb out of sand.

449. Decoy Tools

Difficulty 2/5

Project Outline:

Allow the player to place an instance that will distract enemies for a short time.

Useful Functions and Built-in Variables:

mouse_check_button_*
instance_exists
instance_create_layer
draw_healthbar

Hints on Tackling This Assignment:

Allow player to click to place a decoy, that counts down, showing hp as a bar, and destroys when done. When present, enemy to attack the decoy instead of player.

GAMEMAKER PROGRAMMING CHALLENGES

Difficulty
1/5

450. Colourful Explosions

Project Outline:

To cover the screen with an assortment of colourful effects.

Useful Functions and Built-in Variables:

mouse_check_button_*
repeat
irandom_range
choose
effect_create_layer

Hints on Tackling This Assignment:

Use repeat to make 100 effects. Select a random position in room, along with a random effect type and colour.

451. Fighting Game Knockback

Difficulty 3/5

Project Outline:

To develop a system so that when attacked, the character moves backwards, then recovers.

Useful Functions and Built-in Variables:

sprite_index
image_index
x
enum

Hints on Tackling This Assignment:

If player is hit, change to a hit state. Move back quickly during hit state. When state returns to idle, slowly move back to start position. Use animation end event to change state back to idle.

452. Enemy Mirrors Player

Project Outline:

To make an enemy that moves in sync with the player.

Useful Functions and Built-in Variables:

draw_sprite_ext

Hints on Tackling This Assignment:

Create an enemy that mimics the player movement and position by getting the player's position and current sprite.

GAMEMAKER PROGRAMMING CHALLENGES

Difficulty
2/5

453. Random Direction Movement

Project Outline:

Make a system where an enemy periodically changes direction.

Useful Functions and Built-in Variables:

alarm
direction
irandom

Hints on Tackling This Assignment:

Use an alarm that retriggers. When it does set direction as a random value. On collision with room border, reverse direction.

454. Enemy Swoop Attack

Difficulty 3/5

Project Outline:

To set up an enemy so that it swoops in, fires a barrage of weapons, then retreats.

Useful Functions and Built-in Variables:

```
enum
distance_to_point
move_towards_point
instance_create_layer
```

Hints on Tackling This Assignment:

Periodically set an alarm. If idle state move towards player, fire a sortie of weapons and retreat, resetting alarm.

455. Cluster Bombs

Difficulty 3/5

Project Outline:

To create a weapon spread that splits into smaller weapons.

Useful Functions and Built-in Variables:

`instance_create_layer`
`for`
`instance_destroy`

Hints on Tackling This Assignment:

On mouse click create a spread of weapons moving at equal angles, using a for loop. Set an alarm for weapon, when it triggers create extra mini weapons that spread out.

Difficulty
1/5

456. Synchronized Movement

Project Outline:

To develop a system where all enemies move in sync, using paths

Useful Functions and Built-in Variables:

`path_start`

Hints on Tackling This Assignment:

Create several enemies that start on the same path relative to starting point, at different positions.

GAMEMAKER PROGRAMMING CHALLENGES

Difficulty
3/5

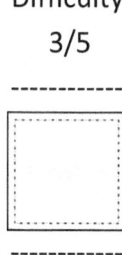

457. Spring-Loaded Enemies

Project Outline:

To create a system so that when a player gets close to an enemy, the enemy starts jumping.

Useful Functions and Built-in Variables:

alarm
distance_to_object
vspeed

Hints on Tackling This Assignment:

Set an alarm for enemy that retriggers. If player is within range when alarm triggers, make it move up and then fall back down.

GAMEMAKER PROGRAMMING CHALLENGES

Difficulty
3/5

458. Gap Crossers

Project Outline:

To create a system where an enemy can identify a gap and jump across it.

Useful Functions and Built-in Variables:

place_meeting
vspeed
gravity

Hints on Tackling This Assignment:

Look for a floor in the direction the enemy is moving. If there is no floor then make the instance jump over the gap.

Difficulty 3/5

459. Slime Trails

Project Outline:

When an enemy moves, create a slime trail that slows down the player.

Useful Functions and Built-in Variables:

```
alarm
instance_create_layer
draw_sprite_ext
```

Hints on Tackling This Assignment:

Set enemy on a path and set an alarm. On alarm, create a slime instance and retrigger. Slowly fade the slime away. If player walks on slime, slow down movement.

460. Change Path Direction

Project Outline:

To create an enemy that follows a path, randomly changing direction and speed.

Useful Functions and Built-in Variables:

irandom_range
path_start
path_speed

Hints on Tackling This Assignment:

Start a path and set an alarm. When it triggers, restart and set a positive or negative value to this. Set the path speed value so it periodically changes direction.

Difficulty
3/5

461. Spiral Dive

Project Outline:

Create an enemy that rotates around the player, gradually getting closer, when within a certain distance, start moving away, and then repeat.

Useful Functions and Built-in Variables:

```
point_direction
distance_to_point
lengthdir_*
```

Hints on Tackling This Assignment:

At start of enemy set start distance and angle to player. Gradually reduce distance until it reaches a min distance, then slowly increase distance, then repeat. Use a variable for angle that increases to orbit the player.

GAMEMAKER PROGRAMMING CHALLENGES

Difficulty
3/5

462. Ambush Hunters

Project Outline:

To create an enemy that hides behind a crate, and periodically pops out to attack the player.

Useful Functions and Built-in Variables:

`enum`
`irandom_range`
`distance_to_object`

Hints on Tackling This Assignment:

Set up with enemies hiding behind a crate. Set an alarm for random duration. When alarm triggers, attack the player.

**Difficulty
3/5**

463. Healers

Project Outline:

To develop a system where enemies are healed by another entity when their health drops below a certain level.

Useful Functions and Built-in Variables:

alarm
instance_exists
point_distance
move_towards_point
with

Hints on Tackling This Assignment:

Use an alarm to periodically look for enemies that have hp below 100. If it finds one, move towards it, and when in contact with it increase the enemy's hp.

Difficulty 3/5

464. Charging Enemies

Project Outline:

To show visually an enemy charging up, before unleashing a sortie of weapons.

Useful Functions and Built-in Variables:

for
instance_create_layer
lengthdir_*

Hints on Tackling This Assignment:

Set enemy with a charge variable that slowly increases to 100. Draw this as a circular bar around enemy. When fully charged start shooting a sortie of bullets.

Difficulty
3/5

465. Dodging Enemies

Project Outline:

Create an enemy that tries to avoid player projectiles by moving in a random direction when a player's bullet exists.

Useful Functions and Built-in Variables:

enum
distance_to_point
move_towards_point
instance_exists
choose

Hints on Tackling This Assignment:

Set an alarm that re-triggers. If a player weapon exists when alarm triggers, move in a random direction.

GAMEMAKER PROGRAMMING CHALLENGES

Difficulty
3/5

466. Orbital Shields

Project Outline:

To develop a system where enemies have shields that rotate around them

Useful Functions and Built-in Variables:

for
lengthdir_*
instance_create_layer
point_direction

Hints on Tackling This Assignment:

Use a for loop to spawn equally spaced shield instances around player. Rotate around the player by increasing a variable for the angle and lengthdir_*.

467. Swing Enemies

Difficulty 3/5

Project Outline:

To create an enemy that swings on a rope.

Useful Functions and Built-in Variables:

enum
draw_sprite_ext
lengthdir_*

Hints on Tackling This Assignment:

Use an enum state to keep track of direction swinging. Use a rope length with lengthdir_* to calculate position. Draw a rope from anchor to position.

GAMEMAKER PROGRAMMING CHALLENGES

Difficulty
3/5

468. Hiding Enemies

Project Outline:

Make an enemy that seeks out a position behind a crate so player cannot see it. Periodically drops bombs as it moves.

Useful Functions and Built-in Variables:

```
mp_grid_*
irandom
path_start
collision_line
```

Hints on Tackling This Assignment:

Set up an mp_grid and add crates to it. Set enemy to look for a location to hide from player, by looking at random positions until one if found with crate in the way. Randomly drop bombs when moving.

469. Directional Blockers

Difficulty 4/5

Project Outline:

Create enemies that move around and block the player's movement.

Useful Functions and Built-in Variables:

mp_grid_*
instance_find
path_start
instance_find

Hints on Tackling This Assignment:

Create a grid based layout. Set up some crates to randomly move to a preset position. Set an alarm and repeat. Prevent player from moving through crates.

GAMEMAKER PROGRAMMING CHALLENGES

Difficulty
2/5

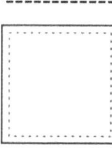

470. Sky Divers

Project Outline:

To create enemies that drop in and retreat.

Useful Functions and Built-in Variables:

vspeed
mouse_check_button_*

Hints on Tackling This Assignment:

Start instance above room, then use a large vspeed value to drop quickly. When target reached, set vspeed to small negative value to slowly move up.

471. Split Creatures

Difficulty 3/5

Project Outline:

To split enemies into smaller instances of themselves when destroyed.

Useful Functions and Built-in Variables:

path_start
draw_healthbar
instance_create_layer
instance_destroy

Hints on Tackling This Assignment:

Set an enemy with hp, and moving on a path. When clicked reduce hp. When no hp spawn a number of mini enemies to expand from its position, then follow a path.

Difficulty
1/5

472. Barrel Rolls

Project Outline:

To create an animation control that allows the player to perform a barrel roll.

Useful Functions and Built-in Variables:

mouse_check_button_*
sprite_index
image_index

Hints on Tackling This Assignment:

Allow input to change the sprite to roll animation.
When animation is finished, reset to starting sprite.
Use a flag to prevent rolling if already rolling.

473. Dogfight Lock-On

Project Outline:

Create a system that allows player to lock-on to an enemy and show this visually.

Useful Functions and Built-in Variables:

alarm
draw_sprite
mouse_check_button_*
point_direction

Hints on Tackling This Assignment:

Lock-on to the nearest enemy of mouse position.
When mouse is clicked, shoot a bullet towards target.

GAMEMAKER PROGRAMMING CHALLENGES

Difficulty
3/5

474. Cloud Cover Stealth

Project Outline:

Create a system so an enemy can't detect a player when hiding in a cloud.

Useful Functions and Built-in Variables:

place_meeting
instance_create_layer
alarm

Hints on Tackling This Assignment:

Use a global flag that is true when player is in a cloud. Set up the enemy to move to player's y position and fire a bullet when player is not hidden.

Difficulty
2/5

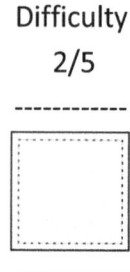

475. Plane Switching

Project Outline:

To allow the player to switch between planes that have different abilities.

Useful Functions and Built-in Variables:

mouse_wheel_*
keyboard_check

Hints on Tackling This Assignment:

Create a plane with different coloured planes as subimges. Allow mouse wheel to change plane. Depending on plane, move quicker, fire bullets or better fuel economy.

476. Colour Matching

Project Outline:

To allow the player to change colour so it can move within a coloured area.

Useful Functions and Built-in Variables:

```
image_speed
image_index
mouse_wheel_*
keyboard_check
instance_place
```

Hints on Tackling This Assignment:

Allow player to change colour (changing sprite subimage) and only movement through a zone of the same colour, by only allowing movement if colours match.

477. Mine Weapon

Difficulty 3/5

Project Outline:

To create a weapon that starts a countdown when hit by the player.

Useful Functions and Built-in Variables:

effect_create_layer
draw_healthbar

Hints on Tackling This Assignment:

Create a mine with hp and flag for active or not, setting to false. When hit by player start countdown and explode when done. Draw a countdown bar.

478. Mini Helper

Difficulty 4/5

Project Outline:

To create an extra player that can moved and stay in range of the player.

Useful Functions and Built-in Variables:

keyboard_check
place_meeting
point_distance
mp_potential_step

Hints on Tackling This Assignment:

Create a mini player that can be moved with keys. When over a set distance from player, use mp_potential_step to move to player, avoiding instances.

Difficulty
2/5

479. Teleporting Enemies

Project Outline:

To create an enemy that periodically moves to a random position, fading in and out.

Useful Functions and Built-in Variables:

enum
draw_sprite_ext

Hints on Tackling This Assignment:

Use a variable for alpha. Use a state machine to fade in and out. When instance has faded out, move to random position and change state.

GAMEMAKER PROGRAMMING CHALLENGES

Difficulty
2/5

480. Patrolling Guards

Project Outline:

To create an enemy that moves on a randomly chosen path, changing direction if encountering another enemy.

Useful Functions and Built-in Variables:

path_start
alarm
path_speed
irandom_range
choose

Hints on Tackling This Assignment:

Start enemy on a random chosen path. Upon collision with another enemy, reverse direction.

481. Area Explosion

Difficulty 2/5

Project Outline:

To create an enemy that delivers a devastating explosion after a countdown.

Useful Functions and Built-in Variables:

mouse_check_button_*
instance_position
for
lengthdir_*
instance_create_layer

Hints on Tackling This Assignment:

Upon mouse click set a flag and start counting down timer. When triggered create a circle of explosion instances using a for loop and lengthdir_*, then reset.

482. Mirror Shields

Difficulty 3/5

Project Outline:

A projectile that will bounce off an enemy if fired from above a distance from the enemy. Only causes damage if fired in close range,

Useful Functions and Built-in Variables:

move_bounce_all
instance_destroy
effect_create_layer

Hints on Tackling This Assignment:

Count how long a missile has been traveling by incrementing a variable. Allow damage below a certain value, otherwise bounce off.

Difficulty 3/5

483. Harassers

Project Outline:

To create an enemy that constantly moves towards the player, and pushes player on contact.

Useful Functions and Built-in Variables:

move_towards_point
point_direction
with
direction
friction

Hints on Tackling This Assignment:

Make an enemy move to player with move_towards_point. Upon collision with player, make the player move in the direction of the enemy. Use friction in player to make at slow down.

484. Spinning Dashers

Project Outline:

To create an enemy that charges up by rotating, before attacking.

Useful Functions and Built-in Variables:

```
move_towards_point
distance_to_point
image_angle
enum
```

Hints on Tackling This Assignment:

Use an enum state machine to control enemy. Make it spin faster and faster, then move to player, retreat and spin down, then repeat.

485. Laser Sweepers

Difficulty 3/5

Project Outline:

To make a laser that penetrates enemies and displays an effect when hitting them.

Useful Functions and Built-in Variables:

lengthdir_*
position_meeting
effect_create_layer
for

Hints on Tackling This Assignment:

Make a laser that rotates. Use a for loop and lengthdir_* to check for enemy along laser direction. Create an effect if enemy is at that position.

GAMEMAKER PROGRAMMING CHALLENGES

Difficulty
3/5

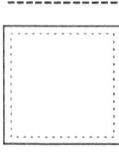

486. Ground Pounders

Project Outline:

To make enemies jump, upon landing they damage a player if within a range.

Useful Functions and Built-in Variables:

move_and_collide
ds_list_create
ds_list_size
position_meeting
instance_create_layer

Hints on Tackling This Assignment:

Create an enemy that uses an alarm to jump. On collision with floor set floor instances in range to active. If player is standing on active floor, apply damage.

487. Mini Map Level Selection

Difficulty 4/5

Project Outline:

Create a path the player can manually move on, as a means for level selection.

Useful Functions and Built-in Variables:

path_get_length
mouse_check_button
path_get_x
path_get_y
instance_position

Hints on Tackling This Assignment:

Create a path, move along it using mouse buttons.
Draw a sprite at current position with path_get_*.
Add some places on path and draw info upon collision.

GAMEMAKER PROGRAMMING CHALLENGES

Difficulty
4/5

488. Replenish Stats

Project Outline:

Allow player to collect food, water and firewood to replenish stats.

Useful Functions and Built-in Variables:

clamp
position_meeting

Hints on Tackling This Assignment:

Create some variables for food, water and wood that slowly reduce. When player collides with an item placed in room. replenish that variable.

489. Player Decoy

Difficulty 2/5

Project Outline:

Allow player to place a decoy that attracts the enemy.

Useful Functions and Built-in Variables:

mouse_check_button_*
instance_exists alarm
instance_create_layer
distance_to_point
move_towards_point

Hints on Tackling This Assignment:

On mouse click create a decoy if one doesn't already exist. Set an alarm that counts down to destroy it. Make enemy target decoy instead of player.

Difficulty
2/5

490. Variable Damage

Project Outline:

To make a system that creates damage relative to speed when hitting an instance.

Useful Functions and Built-in Variables:

health
keyboard_check
place_meeting
abs

Hints on Tackling This Assignment:

Create a movement system that makes a player move left and right, getting faster as key is held down. On collision reduce health according to the speed.

491. Solar Flares

Difficulty 3/5

Project Outline:

To make a sun that randomly expands and reduces size. If the Sun touches a character, the character takes damage.

Useful Functions and Built-in Variables:

enum
irandom_range
point_distance

Hints on Tackling This Assignment:

Use an alarm to change a state to make a sun increase in size and then shrink back. If the Sun touches a character, reduce its hp.

Difficulty 2/5

492. Zombie Enemy

Project Outline:

To create an enemy that cannot be killed, that always moves towards the player.

Useful Functions and Built-in Variables:

distance_to_object
move_towards_point
image_angle
point_direction

Hints on Tackling This Assignment:

Make an enemy that constantly move towards player. Use image_angle to point towards the player, and move in that direction.

493. Surround Player

Difficulty 3/5

Project Outline:

To make enemies surround a player at a distance, and move with some randomness.

Useful Functions and Built-in Variables:

irandom
lengthdir_*
move_towards_point
distance_to_point
collision_line

Hints on Tackling This Assignment:

Make enemies hover around the player by moving to a target point near the player.

GAMEMAKER PROGRAMMING CHALLENGES

Difficulty
3/5

494. Enemy Hint

Project Outline:

Create a sprite indicator pointing to the direction of an incoming enemy.

Useful Functions and Built-in Variables:

`with`
`point_direction`
`draw_sprite_ext`

Hints on Tackling This Assignment:

Check if an enemy is outside the view. If it is draw an indicator next to the player, pointing to the direction of the enemy.

495. Power Upgrade

Difficulty 3/5

Project Outline:

To allow an upgrade of all towers within a given range.

Useful Functions and Built-in Variables:

```
distance_to_point
with
for
draw_circle
draw_rectangle
```

Hints on Tackling This Assignment:

Create a controller object that moves with mouse and draws a circle showing range. On click upgrade towers in range, and draw level above tower.

Difficulty
3/5

496. Electricity Towers

Project Outline:

To allow placement of 2 towers that make electricity between them.

Useful Functions and Built-in Variables:

mouse_check_button_*
instance_create_layer
mouse_x
mouse_y
draw_line_width

Hints on Tackling This Assignment:

Allow user to click and place a tower, storing the id. On next click make second tower, then draw a line (electricity) between both towers.

497. Freeze Bullets

Difficulty 3/5

Project Outline:

Create an enemy that shoots a bullet at the player which freezes movement for a set amount of time.

Useful Functions and Built-in Variables:

alarm
draw_sprite_ext
mouse_check_button

Hints on Tackling This Assignment:

Use a flag to determine if player is frozen or not. When hit by an enemy bullet, change flag to stop moving and set an alarm. When alarm triggers allow moving again.

GAMEMAKER PROGRAMMING CHALLENGES

Difficulty
3/5

498. Money Based Upgrades

Project Outline:

Allow player to use available cash to upgrade weapon towers and show level visually.

Useful Functions and Built-in Variables:

mouse_check_button_*
instance_position
for
draw_rectangle

Hints on Tackling This Assignment:

Set a variable for the money. When mouse clicked on instance, check if there is enough cash, and - if so - upgrade. Use a for loop to draw coloured rectangles showing hp.

499. Random Paths

Difficulty 1/5

Project Outline:

Make an enemy move on a randomly selected path.

Useful Functions and Built-in Variables:

choose
path_start

Hints on Tackling This Assignment:

Select a path from a random selection using choose and start on path. At end of path repeat.

GAMEMAKER PROGRAMMING CHALLENGES

Difficulty
3/5

500. Reinforcement Callers

Project Outline:

When the enemy hp goes below a value, make other enemies move in to help.

Useful Functions and Built-in Variables:

place_meeting
point_distance
with
move_towards_point

Hints on Tackling This Assignment:

Use point_distance to find enemies within range, and get enemy with lowest hp. If below a threshold, move towards it and keep a distance.

See text file in assets download for sources of assets used in the example projects.

Creative Commons:

Includes Resources Released Under Creative Commons

CC0 1.0

Deed

Canonical URL

https://creativecommons.org/publicdomain/zero/1.0/

See the legal code

No Copyright

The person who associated a work with this deed has dedicated the work to the public domain by waiving all of his or her rights to the work worldwide under copyright law, including all related and neighboring rights, to the extent allowed by law.

You can copy, modify, distribute and perform the work, even for commercial purposes, all without asking permission. See Other Information below.

Other Information

In no way are the patent or trademark rights of any person affected by CC0, nor are the rights that other persons may have in the work or in how the work is used, such as publicity or privacy rights.

Unless expressly stated otherwise, the person who associated a work with this deed makes no warranties about the work, and disclaims liability for all uses of the work, to the fullest extent permitted by applicable law.

When using or citing the work, you should not imply endorsement by the author or the affirmer.

CC BY 3.0

Deed

Notice

This is an older version of this license. Compared to previous versions, the 4.0 versions of all CC licenses are more user-friendly and more internationally robust . If you are licensing your own work , we strongly recommend the use of the 4.0 license instead: Deed - Attribution 4.0

International

Canonical URL

https://creativecommons.org/licenses/by/3.0/

See the legal code

You are free to:

Share — copy and redistribute the material in any medium or format for any purpose, even commercially.

Adapt — remix, transform, and build upon the material for any purpose, even commercially.

The licensor cannot revoke these freedoms as long as you follow the license terms.

Under the following terms:

Attribution — You must give appropriate credit , provide a link to the license, and indicate if changes were made . You may do so in any reasonable manner, but not in any way that suggests the licensor endorses you or your use.

No additional restrictions — You may not apply legal terms or technological measures that legally restrict others from doing anything the license permits.

Notices:

You do not have to comply with the license for elements of the material in the public domain or where your use is permitted by an applicable exception or limitation . No warranties are given. The license may not give you all of the permissions necessary for your intended use. For example, other rights such as publicity, privacy, or moral rights may limit how you use the material.

GPSR Compliance

The European Union's (EU) General Product Safety Regulation (GPSR) is a set of rules that requires consumer products to be safe and our obligations to ensure this.

If you have any concerns about our products, you can contact us on

ProductSafety@springernature.com

In case Publisher is established outside the EU, the EU authorized representative is:

Springer Nature Customer Service Center GmbH
Europaplatz 3
69115 Heidelberg, Germany

www.ingramcontent.com/pod-product-compliance
Lightning Source LLC
LaVergne TN
LVHW081345060526
838201LV00050B/1711